C0-AVO-091

Tudor and Stuart Texts

The Trial of Nicholas Throckmorton

Tudor and Stuart Texts

Series editors

DAVID GALBRAITH
Department of English, University of Toronto

GERMAINE WARKENTIN
Department of English, University of Toronto

This is a series of modernized scholarly editions of important English Renaissance and Reformation texts, published by the Centre for Reformation and Renaissance Studies. The series emphasises texts which have not been produced in modern editions and whose availability will contribute to ongoing attempts to interpret and to teach the English Renaissance.

Titles published

The True Law of Free Monarchies and *Basilikon Doron*
JAMES I. Ed. Daniel Fischlin and Mark Fortier

The Trial of Nicholas Throckmorton
Ed. Annabel Patterson

For a list of CRRS publications see page 109.

The Trial of Nicholas Throckmorton

A modernized edition

Edited, with an Introduction,
Appendices, and Notes by
Annabel Patterson

Toronto
Centre for Reformation and Renaissance Studies
1998

CRRS Publications
Centre for Reformation and Renaissance Studies
Victoria University in the University of Toronto
Toronto, Canada M5S 1K7

© 1998 by the Centre for Reformation and Renaissance Studies

All rights reserved.

Canadian Cataloguing in Publication Data

Throckmorton, Nicholas, 1515–1571
    The trial of Nicholas Throckmorton

(Tudor and Stuart texts)
A modernized ed.
Includes bibliographical references.
ISBN 0-9697512-8-1

1. Throckmorton, Nicholas, 1515–1571 – Trials, litigation, etc. 2. Trials
(Treason) – England – Early works to 1800. I. Patterson, Annabel M.
II. Victoria University (Toronto, Ont.). Centre for Reformation and
Renaissance Studies. III. Title. IV. Series.

KD372.T47T47 1998   345.42′0231   C98-931805-2

No part of this book may be translated or reproduced in any form, by print,
photoprint, microfilm, or any other means, without written permission
from the publisher.

KD
372
.T46
T47
1998

Contents

Cover illustration: Sir Nicholas Throckmorton (artist unknown), 1562. By courtesy of the National Portrait Gallery, London

Introduction

On July 6, 1553, King Edward VI, the only son of Henry VIII, died of tuberculosis at the sad age of sixteen, and England, or rather the handful of aristocratic families who constituted its governing class, was embroiled in a short but sharp struggle over the succession. In addition to the usual dynastic factionalism, this was driven by disturbances unleashed in England by Henry VIII's quarrel with the Pope and his separation of the English church from Roman Catholic control. Though Henry's momentous changes had been more a matter of marital expediency than any sympathy with the reforms promoted by Martin Luther, the new doctrines had in fact penetrated quite deeply into England, and Edward had been brought up and directed during his short reign by Protestant courtiers, who tried desperately and unsuccessfully to prevent his Roman Catholic elder sister, Mary Tudor, from succeeding him. Mary's Protestant rival, Lady Jane Grey, (also sixteen years old), proclaimed queen by the duke of Northumberland but displaced in just a few days, would be executed on February 12, 1554, her fate sealed by what happened in the interim: the failed rebellion of Sir Thomas Wyatt the younger against the new queen, and particularly against her planned marriage to Philip II of Spain.

Wyatt and other military leaders of the conspiracy were, of course, tried and executed; but there was also a group of eight members of the gentry who were charged with conspiring with Wyatt to seize the Tower of London and levy war against the queen. Of these, two had already escaped to France and four were never brought to trial. The two who were arraigned were Sir James Crofts and Sir Nicholas Throckmorton. David Loades, who gives the most complete account of Wyatt's rebellion, thought that their examinations (none of which has survived) may have been conducted primarily for the purpose of incriminating the princess Elizabeth and Edward Courtenay, earl of Devonshire; and once Throckmorton and Crofts were in custody the Council's interest in the rest of the eight may have waned.[1] In other words, these were exemplary political trials, of considerable importance. The charge was treason. It was all the more astonishing, therefore, when the first defendant, Throckmorton, conducted his defence with such spirit and legal acumen that his jury acquitted him. The chances of this happening in a treason trial in early modern England were worse than slender;[2] but Throckmorton not only managed to outwit the prosecution lawyers by his procedural sophistication, he also apparently persuaded the jury that the law was being unjustly applied and manipulated. The jurors were subsequently imprisoned in the Tower and the Fleet, and fined exorbitantly.

This trial was not only significant in its own day, in terms of Marian history. It was remarkably influential thereafter: as a case to remember in the theory of treason law and trial by jury; as a model for what strategies a defendant might use in such extremity; and also as a model of how and why trial transcripts should be part of public record. The "why" implies such liberal ideas as the value of an educated citizenry and the public's right to know. The "how" includes the manner of record, of transmission and publication, and even, as we shall see, aspects of formal organization and style that belong in the territory of literary history.

The source

The source of the Throckmorton trial was itself unusual, in several ways. It appears as a large insertion in "Holinshed's" *Chronicles*, first published in 1577, at the point where the chronicler had just com-

---

[1] David Loades, *Two Tudor Conspiracies* (Cambridge: Cambridge University Press, 1965), 96–7.

[2] There were precedents, however. See John Bellamy, *The Tudor Law of Treason* (London: Routledge and Kegan Paul, 1989), 171: "A recent study of treason cases in the years 1530–40, admittedly a period involving several insurrections and a very large number of treason trials, has found no fewer than 32 acquittals out of 600 arraignments."

pleted his narrative of Wyatt's rebellion. Raphael Holinshed introduced this material with some self-consciousness:

> But now forsomuch as a copy of the order of Sir Nicholas Throckmorton's
> arraignment hath come into my hands, and that the same may give some
> light to the history of that dangerous rebellion, I have thought it not
> impertinent to insert the same.[3]

The evaluative issue—of whether, and to whom, this insertion
would appear "impertinent" or not—was thus brought to the
reader's consciousness also.

This is the only instance in the *Chronicles* of a major political trial
in which both prosecution and defence are fully represented, so
fully, indeed, that we are given what appears to be a verbatim
transcript of the entire proceedings. The question of whether it
could have been in fact a verbatim transcript, and if so, by whom,
will be considered shortly. But as Holinshed inserted it, the text also
appears to be a reprinting. Its presentation in the *Chronicles* typographically mimics the title page of a pamphlet; and in other
instances where the *Chronicles's* typography does the same thing,
the original pamphlet has survived. Finally, not only does the
fullness of the account suggest evenhandedness; the trial is presented in what we would now recognize as dramatic form, complete
with speech prefixes and occasional stage directions. The "title-
page" itself calls the text a "Dialogue," a provocative term in the
circumstances, and adds that this form was chosen "for the better
understanding of every man's part," an even more interesting suggestion. But that the idea of drama was formally in the minds of
those who produced this text is also suggested by the fact that
Throckmorton speaks of his trial as a "pageant" and a "woeful
tragedy," and reminds the "lookers-on" that such spectacles have
been common enough on the juridical stage in recent years.

How did this text "come into" Raphael Holinshed's hands? The
chronicler does not tell us, but we can make an educated guess.

---

[3] Raphael Holinshed, *The Chronicles of England, Scotland, and Ireland*, 3
vols., (London, 1587), 3:1104; emphasis added. For a full account of the
Chronicles and their character in both the 1577 and the expanded 1587 editions,
see my *Reading Holinshed's Chronicles* (Chicago: University of Chicago Press,
1994).

John Bellamy, one of the few historians who has recognized its significance, assumed that the account of the trial was probably compiled by Throckmorton himself after Mary's death, though "based on notes taken at the time."[4] But it does not read like the protagonist's reconstruction several years after the event, nor is it told in the first person, as we would expect from personal reconstruction. Rather, the *vraisemblance* of the dialogue and its air of completeness demands one of three possibilities: very extensive notes made at the time by another interested party or parties, since Throckmorton could scarcely have been scribbling while he spoke; subsequent fabrication by someone with a great ear for dialogue and a lively political imagination—a political playwright, as it were; or some combination of the two. Any of these three could have been followed by pamphlet publication; though the non-survival of an original suggests that it was published surreptitiously during Mary's reign, rather than after her death, when such material could have been licensed. Included in this edition is a reprint of what looks like a preface to the trial, produced by the Protestant martyr John Bradford while himself in prison in the summer of 1555. Given the strength of his advertisement for its usefulness, his friends may have been persuaded to risk an illicit publication.

Some skepticism about the "transcript's" accuracy as a verbatim account, or even its truth-content more generally, has been expressed, on the grounds that official transcripts of trials were not produced until the eighteenth century, and shorthand was not used until late in the seventeenth. But in the early fifteenth century ecclesiastical examinations for heresy were taken down in detail by official notaries; and in 1534 unofficial (that is to say, illegal) accounts of the trial of Sir Thomas More were generated, from which several pamphlets were printed abroad. Kitson Clark, who challenged Sir Leslie Stephen's naiveté in the *Dictionary of National Biography* on this matter, nevertheless admitted that Throckmorton's trial "certainly reads as if it were taken down verbatim," and — as one of the possible explanations for its existence — that "it may very well have been reconstructed from the memories of people who had actually been present in the Guildhall at the time of trial, possibly assisted by their notes, possibly assisted by the

---

[4] Bellamy, *Tudor Law of Treason*, 246.

recollections of Sir Nicholas himself."[5] This sounds like an excellent compromise between too much skepticism of the document and too little, and whenever I use the term "transcript," this is the compromise sense I wish it to bear. With regard to its truth-content, the likelihood that Throckmorton did conduct his defence precisely as recorded in the *Chronicles* is supported both by his otherwise surprising acquittal, and the fact that he subsequently had a moderately successful career as a diplomat under Queen Elizabeth I.

But before we turn to Sir Nicholas' biography, one more thing needs to be said about Raphael Holinshed, and his motives for inserting this material in the *Chronicles*. First, its disproportionate length (as compared to the rather brief accounts of the dispatching of Northumberland, Lady Jane Grey, and Wyatt himself) would probably have been noticed, with or without Holinshed's himself raising the question of its possible "impertinence." But in addition to its length, Holinshed drew attention to its special interest, and to what it required of its readers:

> I have thought it not impertinent to insert the same; not wishing that it should be offensive to any, sith [since] it is in every man's liberty to weigh his words uttered in his own defence, and likewise the doings of the quest [inquest,jury] in acquitting him, as may seem good to their discretions, sith I have delivered the same as I have it, without prejudicing any man's opinion to think thereof otherwise than as the cause may move him. (3:1104).

The Elizabethan readers were therefore being encouraged, in effect, themselves to serve as another jury, to use their own capacity for independent and unbiased thought, a qualification ideally assumed in the theory of trial by jury. Throckmorton sought to develop this capacity in his own jurors, particularly with respect to their educability in the most intricate details of the law. Replaying Throckmorton's strategy for his own purposes, Holinshed sought to educate his readers in the ways of the law and particularly in the concept of justice as fairness, a humanist or liberal ideal that Throckmorton himself consistently (and frequently) refers to as "indifference."

---

[5] G.Kitson Clark, *The Critical Historian* (New York: Basic Books, 1967), 95.

But there was also a religious imperative and rhetoric. A large part of Throckmorton's strategy in the opening moments of the trial consisted in a struggle for control over procedure, implying that the accepted rules of procedure were stacked against the defendant, and including the suggestion that "due process" meant taking enough time: "My lords, I pray you," he said, when his judges expressed impatience, "Make not too much haste with me, neither think not long for your dinner, for my case requireth leisure, and you have well dined when you have done justice truly. Christ said, 'Blessed are they that hunger and thirst for righteousness.'" And this citation from Matthew 5:6 was only the first of a series of brilliantly chosen biblical allusions. This was not only to claim the moral high ground, but also a strategy likely to appeal to a jury of London merchants, so many of whom, as Susan Brigden has demonstrated, were the resilient and resourceful core of Protestantism at this time.[6]

Throckmorton particularly invoked those passages, such as Mark's account of the unjust trial of Christ by the Pharisees or Paul's epistle to the Ephesians, which stressed the relation between the persecution of a religion, solidarity in the face of it, and that religion's subsequent validation and triumph. Mark's brief description of the illegal nighttime examination of Christ, the production of the false witnesses, and Pilate's washing of his hands provided one telling analogy. And when at the end of the trial Throckmorton bade farewell to his jury by citing Paul's farewell to the Ephesians, he expected them to remember Paul's request that "utterance may be given unto me, that I may open my mouth boldly, to make known the mystery of the gospel; For which I am an ambassador in bonds." Sir Nicholas Throckmorton, another ambassador in bonds, was an equally gifted communicator.

Sir Nicholas Throckmorton

Throckmorton, who was thirty-seven at the time of his trial, had already had quite a significant career, part courtier and part parliamentarian. Born in 1515, he was one of eight sons of Sir George Throckmorton of Coughton, Warwickshire. His mother was aunt by

---

[6] Susan Brigden, *London and the Reformation* (Oxford: Clarendon Press, 1989).

marriage to Queen Catherine Parr. The sons, caught up in post-Reformation disputes, divided along religious lines. Robert, the eldest, remained like his father a staunch Catholic, and John, the youngest brother but one, though he had drawn the proclamation in favor of Lady Jane Grey, was a quick convert back to the old religion. Two of his sons, Thomas and Francis, were involved in Jesuit conspiracy against Elizabeth, and Francis was executed for treason in May 1585. In contrast, the third son Clement was a radical Protestant, and his son Job was probably the irrepressible author of the radical puritan Marprelate pamphlets. Nicholas himself, with George and Clement, joined the Protestant household of Catherine Parr soon after her marriage to the king in July 1543. With two brothers (probably again George and Clement) he was present as a sympathiser in 1546 at the execution of the Protestant martyr Anne Askew.

Nicholas's career, however, had been and would be entirely secular. He began in court service, as page to the duke of Richmond, Henry's illegitimate son, who died in 1536. Like three of his brothers, Clement, John and Kenelm, he was several times elected to the House of Commons, and from 1545, for over twenty years, he repeatedly sat in parliament for a series of different constituencies. During Edward's VI's reign he made a second entry into court service. In 1547 he accompanied Protector Somerset's army to Scotland, and after the battle of Musselburgh he had brought news of the victory to Edward, who knighted him and appointed him to the privy chamber, the place of nearest access to the king.

Although this period in the sun, dependent as it was on Somerset and the frail young king, was inevitably short lived, Throckmorton seems to have survived Somerset's fall and the chaotic transition to the new reign quite well, walking the political tightrope with only a few wobbles. His signature appears on the letters patent of June 7, 1553, which limited the succession to Lady Jane, but on the day of Edward's death, which Northumberland wished to maintain as a secret until he could consolidate Lady Jane's position, Throckmorton and three of his brothers are said to have sent Mary's goldsmith to inform her of the event so that she would not be taken by surprise. The story has it that Mary, "suspecting Sir Nicholas his Intrigues," asked whether Robert had been author of the message, since then she would have trusted it. Then, when she was proclaimed queen at Northampton by Sir Thomas Tresham, Throckmorton briefly attacked Tresham, and was nearly killed by

Mary's supporters in the town.[7] Seeing which way the wind was blowing, Throckmorton then joined forces with Tresham, and was with him appointed to conduct Mary on her progress to London. As part of her acts of conciliation, Mary granted him some land forfeited by Northampton; but in the 1553 parliament his name appears on a list of members who "stood for the true religion" against the reintroduction of Catholicism in England. It was not entirely surprising, therefore, that on February 20, 1554 he was sent to the Tower, on the testimony of one of Wyatt's lieutenants, Cuthbert Vaughan, that he and Throckmorton had discussed together certain plans for the insurrection. He was tried in the Guildhall on April 17 by a commission of oyer and terminer,[8] after fifty-eight days of close imprisonment.

After his acquittal, Throckmorton was at first retained in the Tower, in the hope that further charges could be brought against him. When released on January 18, 1555, though constrained to obedience by a 2000 pound bond, he retired to his home in Northamptonshire. Then in June 1556 another conspiracy against Mary was discovered, involving another John Throckmorton. Nicholas was alarmed for his own safety. He broke his bond and fled to France, from where, via Sir Henry Wotton, he petitioned the queen for pardon, and apologized for leaving the country without permission.[9] A year later, thanks to the intercession of his brother John, Mary was convinced of his innocence of complicity in this later plot, pardoned him and restored his confiscated property. Upon his return (and perhaps previously) he had established communication with the princess Elizabeth, which was amply rewarded upon *her* succession in 1558. He went on to become a ubiquitous figure in court and diplomatic circles under Elizabeth, negotiating on her behalf in Scotland and France throughout the 1560s, always with a

---

[7] See *The Chronicle of Queen Jane, and two years of Queen Mary ... written by a resident in the Tower of London*, ed. J.G. Nichols (London: Camden Society, 1850), 12. Tresham married into the Catholic wing of the Throckmorton family, his wife being Muriel, Robert's daughter.

[8] Literally, "to hear and conclude," a technical term referring to a high-level criminal trial conducted by a team of the monarch's appointees for this occasion only.

[9] Copies of his letter to Mary exist in British Library mss. Stowe 280 (ff. 104–66) and Add. 33271 (ff. 10–11v.)

zealous Protestant agenda of his own. He expended much energy in the case, and to some extent in the cause, of Mary queen of Scots, whom he tried to persuade to abandon Darnley, and whose projected marriage to Thomas Howard, duke of Norfolk, Throckmorton promoted. Perhaps as a result, in the last year of his life he was arrested on suspicion of involvement in the Northern Rebellion, but was released to die in his bed in February 1571.[10]

Throckmorton himself had married Anne, daughter of Sir Nicholas Carew, and one of his own daughters, Elizabeth, became famous in her own right as the lover and then wife of Sir Walter Ralegh, a bone of contention between Ralegh and the queen, and the model for Serena in the sixth book of Spenser's *Faerie Queene*. In addition to the sources already cited there exists a more questionable source of details about Throckmorton's life: a remarkable poem entitled *The Legend of Sir Nicholas Throckmorton*, in six-line stanzas, imitative of the "lives" in *The Mirror for Magistrates* in that the speaker represents himself as Sir Nicholas himself returned from the grave. This poem, which was edited by the Whig Francis Peck in an appendix to his *Life of Milton* in 1740, and re-edited by J.G. Nichols in 1874, is partially reprinted here. Not only does it contain many intriguing details, some of which bear on the 1554 trial, some of which (such as the charge of being poisoned by the earl of Leicester, in revenge for his having opposed Leicester's marriage to Elizabeth) have been dismissed as pure invention; but along with the texture of the trial itself, and Throckmorton's connections, via Job and Elizabeth, to other events of significance in Elizabethan culture, it serves to remind us of the uneasy boundary between the literary and the historical, a boundary which we need to remember without necessarily the desire (or the resources) to patrol it.

One of the details for which we are indebted to the *Legend* is a glimpse of Throckmorton's personal appearance, as perceived by his contemporaries. In the course of a series of complaints about how he always seemed to miss out on the major appointments at

---

[10] For biographical accounts of Sir Nicholas, see the *Dictionary of National Biography*; A.L. Rowse, *Ralegh and the Throckmortons* (London: MacMillan, 1962), 18–54; S.T. Bindoff, ed. *The House of Commons 1509–1558* (London: Secker & Warburg, 1982), 3:458–460; and P.W. Hasler, ed. *The House of Commons 1558–1603*, 3:497–99.

court, the "ghost" complains of his unpopularity, a direct consequence of his closeness to Elizabeth:

> Yet afterwards, if any great demand
> Or suit was made, whereto the Queen said no;
> If once a thing misliked she did command,
> Into a common by-word it did grow,
> That weasel-face Throckmorton had been there.
> So I, though guiltless, all the blame did bear. (Stanza 176)

The splendid portrait of Throckmorton reproduced on the cover of this edition does indeed show where the adjective "weasel-face" came from; handsome, sinister, undeniably wary, looking sideways at an unseen threat or companion.

In that spirit, I cannot resist adding a detail that derives from oral history via the *Legend's* first editor, Francis Peck. "I have been informed," wrote Peck in his appendix to the *Life of Milton*:

> that when Sir Nicholas Throckmorton was poisoned as aforesaid, & lay upon his death-bed at Leicester House, he called one of his own gentlemen privately to him, & charged him, "When I am dead and gone," said he, "tell that rogue Leicester that I say, he hath poisoned me; but that I hope my daughter Betty Raleigh, will outlive him, & (when he is also dead & gone) lift up her vardingal[11] & piss upon his grave. And tell her from me, that I charge her, if possible, to do so.[12]

Peck also reported that one of Sir Nicholas's descendants carried out this charge on a regular basis. Whatever its truth-content, the anecdote is worthy of the man whose trial is reprinted here, whose sense of the ridiculous was one of his most effective weapons, and whose gifts for satire at the right moment were able to transform a potential tragedy of state into a comedy of manners.

Tudor treason law

But one cannot fully appreciate Throckmorton's brilliance without some understanding of the history of treason law in the Tudor

---

[11] Farthingale: a hooped petticoat.

[12] Francis Peck, *New Memoirs of the Life and Poetical Works of Mr. John Milton* (London, 1740), 59.

period. The most complete introduction to this topic is John Bellamy's *The Tudor Law of Treason*, which several times uses Throckmorton's trial as an illustration. Bellamy demonstrated that the Tudor period was one of rapid and arbitrary legal innovation, during which the definition of treason expanded to meet the local and contingent needs of particular monarchs. Treason (from the Norman *trahison*, betrayal), breaking one's allegiance to monarch or state, was the highest secular crime. In 1352, the basic treason statute devised by and for Edward III (25 Edw. 3 ch. 2) defined the crime as compassing or imagining the king's death (or that of his nearest and dearest), levying war in his dominions, and/or assisting his enemies. Throughout the late medieval period, scarcely an untroubled era politically, the Yorkist and Lancastrian dynasties were content with this already broad but action-oriented definition. However, the policies of Henry VIII, which resulted in his divorce from Katherine of Aragon and his break with the papacy, created new kinds of disturbances, and new needs for state control. In November 1534, Henry introduced his own Treason Act (26 Hen. 8 ch. 13), which identified three brand-new treasons. It was now held treason either to express maliciously in speech or writing a desire or intention to endanger or depose the monarch and his immediate family, or "to call the King, in express writing or words, slanderously and maliciously, a heretic, schismatic, tyrant, infidel, or a usurper of the crown."[13] Thus political and religious disagreement, which to modern eyes is scarcely *de facto* malicious, was now explicitly labelled treason; and the failure to report it was misprision of treason.

Bellamy also remarked, however, that whereas each of the Tudors expanded the scope of treason during the course of their reigns, expansion was not continuous. On the contrary, contractions tended to occur at the beginning of reigns, "when a new monarch, probably in search of additional popularity, ... removed the most disliked features of the law which his predecessor had operated," (p. 47). Thus at the beginning of the young king Edward VI's reign, a new treason act (1 Edw. 6 ch. 12) began by describing

---

[13] See G.R. Elton, *Policy and Police: The Enforcement of the Reformation in the Age of Thomas Cromwell* (Cambridge: Cambridge University Press, 1972), 287, 499–400.

the Henrician act as "very straight, sore, extreme and terrible," and then enacted a partial return to the statute of 1352.[14] It remained treason to challenge the royal supremacy over the church or the monarch's legitimacy; but if these challenges were only verbal, and not written or translated into overt action, they were only to be treasonable on the third offence. And when Mary Tudor came to the throne, though her first opponents were tried under the acts of Edward III and Edward VI, she too introduced a treason statute of her own, (I. Mar. 1 ch. 1) in which she outdid her brother in committing herself to abide by the treason law of Edward III alone. In particular, the preamble to her statute focused on the fact that many of the nobility and gentry "have of late (for words only, without other opinion, fact or deed) suffered shameful death not accustomed to nobles," and "that the severity of such like extreme, dangerous and painful laws" was to be abandoned, as against the queen's will and character. It was this confusing situation that Sir Nicholas Throckmorton and his judges inherited; and it was Throckmorton, rather than his judges, who was able to turn to his advantage the self-contradictions—indeed, the political expediency—of the law as exposed by its recent history.

One of the central points that Throckmorton made was that under the new Marian statute, by which treason law reverted to that of Edward III, mere conversations, which were all that could be proven against him as to the charge of complicity (or worse, of masterminding the whole conspiracy) were no longer treason. He had effectively been indicted under a statute no longer in force. Conspiring or "devising" to levy war, as distinct from actually levying it, was not even treason by the medieval definition. The crown's lawyers inexplicably failed to make full use of the fairly flexible concept of "imagining the queen's death," and thus opened themselves to the charge of illegal procedure.

Evidently Raphael Holinshed, always interested in the law, regarded this statutory instability as particularly worthy of his

---

[14] Rather charmingly, the Edwardian statute, certainly composed by Somerset, remarked on the change in the political climate: "But, as in tempest or winter one course and garment is convenient, in calm or warm weather a more liberal race or lighter garment both may and ought to be followed and used." See G.R. Elton, *The Tudor Constitution* (Cambridge: Cambridge University Press, 1960, 2nd. ed. 1982), 65.

readers' attention. At the point in the trial where Throckmorton was pressing his advantage on the basis of the Marian statute, Holinshed remarked in the margin: "Happy for Throckmorton that those statutes stood then repealed." And at the end of the "transcript," he added his own summary:

> Thus much for Sir Nicholas Throckmorton's arraignment, wherein is to be considered, that the repealing of certain statutes in the last parliament was the chief matter he had to allege for his advantage; whereas the repealing of the same statutes was meant notwithstanding for another purpose (as before you have partly heard), which statutes or the effect of the chief branches of them have been since that time again revived, as by the books of the statutes it may better appear, to the which I refer the reader (3:1117).

It would be possible to read this comment as a warning against any enjoyment of Throckmorton's escape, a reminder that he was able, perhaps improperly, to take advantage of a loophole in the law that had now, under Elizabeth, been properly closed. It would be equally possible to read it as an ironic reflection on the severity of the Elizabethan treason statute of 1572, a severity that even her sister of the persecuting reputation had publicly (if briefly) repudiated.[15]

But a modern reader may also be puzzled—not to say shocked— by what this trial shows us of early modern judicial *procedure* in a treason trial. The most striking feature of such trials, from our perspective, is that the defendant was not permitted legal counsel in court, but was required to speak for himself. This rule persisted until altered by a statute of William III in 1696 (2 & 8 Will. 3 ch. 3). The articulated rationale was that, since the defendant had acted against the monarch, anyone who spoke on his behalf would also be a traitor; the unspoken and archaic rationale was that the accused would, as in earlier rituals such as the ordeal, inevitably reveal his own guilt, that self-defence would serve as a form of confession. The distinction between unintentional self-incrimination and con-

---

[15] Immediately after Throckmorton's acquittal, in November 1554, however, Mary issued a new and more severe treason act (1 & 2 Philip and Mary , c.9), which returned mere words against her or King Philip, including prayers, to the category of treason.

fession could be made (Throckmorton in fact made it), but it was not to be formally recognized until very much later.

As late as 1689, in fact, Sir John Hawles (who became William's Attorney General) published an account of Tudor and Stuart juridical practice in cases of treason which gives a horrifically clear picture of what Throckmorton faced—and what law reform, especially in the American Bill of Rights, particularly addressed. As Hawles remarked, commenting on the trials under Charles II of William Lord Russell and Algernon Sidney, among others:

> a man is by a messenger, without any indictment precedent, which by the common law ought to precede, or any accuser or accusation that he knows of, clapt up in close prison, and neither friend nor relation must come to him, he must have neither pen, ink or paper, or know of what, or by whom he is accused. ... If any person advise or solicit for him, unless assigned by the court by which he is tried, they are punishable: he is tried as soon as he comes into the court, and therefore of a solicitor there is no occasion or use. ... The prisoner indeed hath liberty to except to thirty-five of the jury peremptorily, and as many more as he hath cause to except to, but he must not know beforehand who the jury are; but the king's counsel must have a copy of them ... there is a proclamation to call in all persons to swear against him, none is permitted to swear for him; all the impertinent evidence that can be given is permitted against him, none for him; as many counsel as can be hired are allowed against him, none for him. Let any person consider these circumstances, and it is a wonder how any person escapes: it is downright tying a man's hands behind him, and baiting him to death. ... The trial of Ordeal, of walking between hot bars blindfold, which was abolished for the unreasonableness of it, though it had its [biblical] saying for it too, that God would lead the blind so as not to be burnt if he were innocent, was a much more advantageous trial for the suspected than what was of late practised, where it was ten to one that the accused did not escape.[16]

Despite these odds, the drama of the queen vs. Sir Nicholas Throckmorton unfolded, as we shall see, as a potential tragedy transformed by the wit and intelligence of the protagonist into a political comedy of manners.

---

[16] Cited from *A Complete Collection of State Trials*, ed. T.B. Howell, 21 vols., (London, 1816), 8:733–4.

The aftermath

The afterlife of the Throckmorton trial falls into two distinct phases; an immediate set of consequences for the jurors, and a far-reaching influence on subsequent trials, especially in the later seventeenth century, as also on the manner of their recording in the seventeenth and eighteenth centuries.

First, with respect to the jurors. After their unsatisfactory verdict, they were required, on a recognizance (bond) of five hundred pounds apiece, to appear before the Star Chamber on April 21, and after questioning they were committed to prison: Lucar and Whetston, the two alternates who had been added after the challenges and who had emerged as the most courageous, to the Tower, and the others to the Fleet. Under this pressure, four of the jurors, Low, Painter, Bestwick and Cater, submitted and confessed they had erred in their verdict. The remaining eight were called back to the Star Chamber on October 26, 1554, where Lucar "said openly before all the lords they they had done in the matter like honest men, and true and faithful subjects," (3:1121–2). "The Lords taking their words in marvellous evil part," they were sentenced to pay what Holinshed described as "excessive fines," 2,000 pounds apiece for Whetston, Lucar and Keightley, and 1,000 marks apiece for each of the others. In the margin of the 1587 edition, one of the editors, probably John Stow, added his own evaluative comment: "The hard judgement of the lords against those eight honest men."

But Holinshed's own interest in the fate of the jury can be inferred from the fact that he returned to their case a few pages later. On December 12, 1554, he reported, a more realistic compromise was reached. Five of the men in the Fleet:

> were discharged and set at liberty upon their fines paid, which was two hundred and twenty pounds apiece. The other three put up a supplication, therein declaring their goods did not amount to the sum of that which they were appointed to pay: and so upon that declaration, paying three score pounds apiece, they were delivered out of prison on Saint Thomas's day before Christmas, being the one and twentieth day of December. (3:1126)

And, he added significantly, the very next day the first parliament of Philip and Mary was dissolved, having among other legislation passed the statute *ex officio* (to which Throckmorton had ominously alluded in his defence), "and other laws made for punishment of heresies ... revived" (3:1126).[17]

The trial and the fate of the jurors evidently registered strongly as paradigmatic at the time. Apart from the known or conjectured existence of several manuscript copies of the "transcript," (see Bibliography) there exists in Emmanuel College, Cambridge, an advertisement for it written by John Bradford *e carcere* (from prison) in 1555; a fragmentary autobiography by Rose Throckmorton, whose second husband was Nicholas's cousin, and who, as a member of the radical Protestant merchant community in London during Mary's reign, remembered how the Throckmorton jurors in the Fleet had helped her husband and brother; and a partly veiled reference to the trial as a memorable scandal in Sir Thomas Smith's *De Republica Anglorum*, published in 1583. These contemporary responses are also reprinted in Appendix B.

In the next century the Throckmorton trial begins to appear as a model for defendants. In 1649 there was published the trial for treason of John Lilburne, the Leveller, indicted by the Long Parliament for his published attacks upon them.[18] Lilburne too was acquitted, in part, it appears, as a result of his study of Throckmorton's tactics. Early in his testimony, Lilburne referred to:

Throgmorton, in Queen Mary's time, who was impeached of higher treason than now I am; and that in the days of the commonly accounted bloodiest and cruellest prince that this many hundred of years hath reigned in England: ... Throgmorton was in this place [the Guildhall] arraigned as a traitor, and enjoyed as much, if not more [procedural] favor,

---

[17] This referred to 1 & 2 Philip and Mary, c. 6, "For the reviving of three statutes made for the punishment of heresies," including the infamous *de heretico comburendo*, initally passed in 1401. The statute *de officio* seems to be a colloquial reference to 1 & 2 Philip and Mary, c.3: "An act against seditious words and rumours," which supposedly merely reinstated two statutes of Richard II, but in fact added a sinister mechanism, whereby justices of the peace were, by the authority of their office, entitled to hear and determine such cases. If so, it must have been being discussed as in some sense pending prior to this parliament, which convened on November 12, and was dissolved on January 16, 1555. Holinshed evidently mistook the Christmas intercession for the dissolution.

[18] *The Triall of Lieut. Collonel J. Lilburne* (Southwark, 1649).

than I have now enjoyed, although his then judges and prosecutor were bent to take away his life.

At this point in the 1649 pamphlet, Lilburne's editor, Clement Walker (who was operating under the pseudonym "Theodorus Verax") drew attention to the source of Throckmorton's trial:

Whose remarkable and excellent defence you may at large read in Hollingshead's Chronicle, in the Life of Queen Mary, which discourse is excellently well worth the speedily reprinting, especially seeing men are made traitors for words, which cruelty Queen Mary abhorred, as may clearly be read in that excellent statute of hers, made in the first year of her reign (21).

And in the same year, William Walwyn, another Leveller leader in prison for his opinions, alluded to the Throckmorton affair as a model of the principle by which the trial by jury was essential to justice as fairness. "Neither I nor my partners in suffering are any whit doubtful of a full and clear vindication, upon a legal trial," wrote Walwyn:

For in my observation of trials I have generally found juries and jurymen to be full of conscience, care, and circumspection, and tenderness in cases of life and death; and I have read very remarkable passages in our Histories; amongst which the case and trial of Throckmorton, in Queen Mary's time, is most remarkable; the consciences of the jury being proof against the opinion of the judges, the rhetoric of the counsel who were great and learned, nay, against the threats of the court, which was then absolute in power and tyranny, and quit the gentleman like true-hearted, well-resolved Englishmen, that valued their consciences above their lives; and I cannot think but these times will afford as much good conscience, as that time of gross ignorance and superstition did.[19]

Much later in the century, in one of the rash of treason trials of 1683 that followed the Exclusion crisis and the discovery of the Rye House plot, Algernon Sidney (cited by Sir John Hawles as a victim

---

[19] William Walwyn, *The Fountain of Slaunder Discovered*, in *The Writings of William Walwyn*, ed. Jack R. McMichael and Barbara Taft (Athens and London: University of Georgia Press, 1989), 374–75. See also Walwyn's defence of the jury system, *Juries Justified* (1651), 433–45.

of a system stacked against the defendant) also studied Throckmorton's trial, and invoked it in his own unsuccessful defence. He had probably discovered it by studying Lilburne's, which had told him where to find it; but not why Throckmorton had succeeded in his defence where Sidney would fail. Sidney appealed to this precedent in attempting to reestablish the concept of the overt act in a charge of treason, as distinct from conspiracy or intention:

> If it be not plainly under one of the two branches, that I have endeavoured to kill the king, or levied war, then 'tis matter of construction, and that belongs to no court, but the parliament. Then, my lord, this hath been adjudged already in Throgmorton's case. There are twenty judgements of parliament, the act of 13. Eliz. that say—

Unfortunately, where Throckmorton would have been able to rehearse, if not twenty, the one that counted, Sidney trailed off into inarticulateness: "I should have somebody to speak for me."[20] Judge Jeffreys was therefore able to drive home his appalling new maxim that "Scribere est agere," ("writing is doing"); and the manuscript of Sidney's *Discourses concerning Government* functioned as the second witness for the prosecution that the government had been unable to secure.

The role of Sidney in the history and theory of liberal thought is far better known that that of Throckmorton.[21] Sidney is still regarded as one of the intellectual progenitors of the American revolution; but he probably would not have become so formative a model had he not assumed the role that Throckmorton declined—the role of the martyr for a political cause whose time had not yet come. And whatever Sidney learned or failed to learn from Throckmorton in terms of legal strategy, those who shared some or all of his political views had certainly learned the political value of the *published* trial

---

[20] See *The Arraignment, Trial, and Condemnation of Algernon Sydney*, in Sidney, *Discourses on Government*, ed. Thomas Hollis (London, 1763), 147.

[21] See Jonathan Scott, *Algernon Sidney and the Restoration Crisis, 1677–1683* (Cambridge: Cambridge University Press, 1991); and Alan Craig Houston, *Algernon Sidney and the Republican Heritage in England and America* (Princeton: Princeton University Press, 1991).

transcript, as a new genre of great educational and emotional power.

Early in the eighteenth century, in 1719, Thomas Salmon brought out (anonymously) the first edition of the *State Trials*, in which the Throckmorton "transcript" was simply reprinted from the second edition of the *Chronicles*. It thereby became, as it were, a canonical text in the legal history of England; one of the earliest and finest members of a series particularly important to a Whig or liberal perspective, which was, of course, transmitted to the American colonies and became part of American revolutionary thought. Unlike most of the *State Trials*, however, Throckmorton's has information to give us that surpasses the territories of legal education and political philosophy, crucial though they are to the civil society. It brings surprisingly fresh news from the past about character and eloquence, about the structural and ritual relationships between the law and the stage, about how the survival instinct works, and especially about the dynamic interdependence of human beings and texts. Throckmorton's amazing powers of recall, combined with Raphael Holinshed's rescue of the trial transcript from oblivion and its subsequent adventures in other men's and women's experience, give real bite to our sometimes sentimental notions of memory. It is a "found" courtroom drama, all the more exhilarating to read because, given the qualifications registered above, it is also as close as we are likely to get to that elusive entity: historical truth.

The Order of Arraignment of Sir Nicholas Throckmorton, Knight, in the Guildhall of London, the Seventeenth Day of April 1554, Expressed in a Dialogue for the Better Understanding of Every Man's Part

The names
of the com-
missioners

Sir Thomas White, knight, lord mayor of London, the earl of Shrewsbury, the earl of Derby, Sir Thomas Bromley, knight, Lord Chief Justice of England, Sir Nicholas Hare, knight, Master of the Rolls, Sir Francis Englefield, knight, Master of the Court of Wards and Liberties, Sir Richard Southwell, knight, one of the Privy Council, Sir Edward Waldegrave, knight, one of the Privy Council, Sir Roger Cholmley, knight, Sir William Portman, knight, one of the justices of the King's Bench, Sir Edward Sanders, knight, one of the justices of the Common Pleas; Master Stanford and Master Dyer, sergeants [at law], Master Edward Griffin, Attorney General, Master Sendall and Peter Tichbourne, clerks of the Crown.[1]

---

[1] In oyer and terminer proceedings, commissioners were appointed *ad hoc*. In this case, the superior judge was Bromley, as Lord Chief Justice of England. Six of the commissioners were in fact members of the Privy Council: George Talbot, earl of Shrewsbury; Edward Stanley, earl of Derby; Sir Nicholas Hare, Sir

The queen's learned counsel gave evidence against the prisoner	*First, after proclamation made, and the commission read, the Lieutenant of the Tower, Master Thomas Bridges, brought the prisoner to the bar: then silence was commanded, and Sendall said to prisoner as followeth:*
Sendall:	Nicholas Throckmorton, knight, hold up thy hand, thou art before this time indicted of high treason, &c: that thou then and there didst falsely and traitorously, &c: conspire and imagine the death of the queen's majesty, &c: and falsely and traitorously didst levy war against the queen within her realm, &c: and also thou wast adherent to the queen's enemies within her realm, giving to them aid and comfort, &c: and falsely and traitorously didst conspire and intend to depose and deprive the queen of her royal estate, and so finally destroy her, &c: and also thou didst falsely and traitorously devise and conclude to take violently the Tower of London, &c. Of all which treasons and every of them in manner and form &c: art thou guilty or not guilty?
Throckmorton:	May it please you, my lords and masters which be authorised by the queen's commission to be judges this day, to give me leave to speak a few words which doth both concern you and me, before I answer to the indictment, and not altogether impertinent[2] to the matter, and then plead to the indictment.
Bromley:	No. The order is not so. You must first plead whether you be guilty or no.

Francis Engelfield, Sir Richard Southwell, and Sir Edward Waldegrave. The last four of these had all been Mary's personal councillors at Framlingham. The remaining figures were all laywers of various ranks, who shared the responsibility for presenting the case for the prosecution.

[2] Throckmorton here anticipated, and no doubt influenced, Holinshed, in calling his testimony "not...impertinent."

Throckmorton:	If that be your order and law, judge accordingly to it.
Hare:	You must first answer to the matter wherewith you are charged, and then you may talk at your pleasure.
Throckmorton:	But things spoken out of place, were as good not spoken.
Bromley:	These be but delays to spend time, therefore answer as the law willeth you.
Throckmorton:	My lords, I pray you make not too much haste with me, neither think not long for your dinner, for my case requireth leisure, and you have well dined when you have done justice truly. Christ said, "Blessed are they that hunger and thirst for righteousness."[3]
Bromley:	I can forbear my dinner as well as you, and care as little as you, peradventure.
Shrewsbury:	Come you hither to check us, Throckmorton? We will not be so used, no, no. I for mine own part have forborne my breakfast, dinner and supper to serve the queen.
Throckmorton:	Yea, my good lord, I know it right well. I meant not to touch your Lordship, for your service and pains is evidently known to all men.
Southwell:	Master Throckmorton, this talk needeth not. We know what we have to do, and you would teach us our duties. You hurt your matter. Go to, go to.
Throckmorton:	Master Southwell, you mistake me. I meant not to teach you, nor none of you, but to remember you of that I trust you all be well instructed in; and so I satisfy myself, sith [since] I shall not speak, thinking you all know what you have to do, or ought to know: so I will answer to the indictment, and do

---

[3] Matthew 5:6.

plead not guilty to the whole, and to every part thereof.

Sendall: How wilt thou be tried?

Throckmorton: Shall I be tried as I would, or as I should?

Bromley: You shall be tried as the law will, and therefore you must say, "By God and by the country."

Throckmorton: Is that your law for me? It is not as I would, but sith you will have it so, I am pleased with it, and do desire to be tried by faithful just men, which more fear God than the world.

THE NAMES OF THE JURORS[4]

Then the jury was called.	Lucar	Low
	Young	Whetston
	Martin	Painter
	Bestwick	Banks
	Barscarfeld	Calthrop
	Kightley	Cater.[5]

What time the attorney[6] went forthwith to Master Cholmley, and showed him the sheriff's return, who, being acquainted with the citizens, knowing the corruptions and dexterities of them in such cases, noted certain to be challenged for the queen (a rare case) and the same men being known to be sufficient and indifferent, that no exceptions were to be taken to them, but only for their upright honesties: notwithstanding, the attorney prompting Sergeant Dyer, the said sergeant challenged one Bacon and another citizen peremp-

---

[4] In the 1587 edition, these names are highlighted typographically by being centered, and set as two columns framed and divided by elaborate scrolls.

[5] In British Library Stowe Ms. 280, fol 76r, there are different versions of some of the jurors' names, e.g. Katerwane instead of Cater, and two first names that do not appear in the *Chronicles*. For their Protestant connections, see Susan Brigden, *London and the Reformation* (Oxford, 1989), 553–54, who gives their names as Whetstone, Banks, Martin, Lowe, Calthorp, Beswick, Kightley, Young, Baskerville, Lucar, Pointer and Cater.

[6] The attorney: i.e. Griffin.

torily for the queen.[7] *Then the prisoner demanded the cause of the challenge. The sergeant answered:*

Dyer: We need not to show you the cause of the challenge for the queen.

Then the inquest was furnished with other honest men, that is to say, Whetston and Lucar. So the prisoner used these words:

Throckmorton: I trust you have not provided for me this day, as in times past I knew another gentleman occupying this woeful place was provided for. It chanced one of the justices upon jealousy of the prisoner's acquittal, for the goodness of his cause, said to another of his companions, a justice, when the jury did appear, "I like not this jury for our purpose, they seem too pitiful and too charitable to condemn the prisoner." "No, no," said the other judge (to wit Cholmley), "I warrant you, they be picked fellows for the nonce. He shall drink of the same cup his fellows have done." I was then a looker-on of the pageant as others be now here; but now, woe is me, I am a player in that woeful tragedy. Well, for these and such other like the black ox hath of late trodden on some of their feet;[8] but my trust is, I shall not be so used.

Whilst this talk was, Cholmley consulted with the attorney about the jury, which the prisoner espied, and then said as here ensueth:

---

[7] Jurors could be challenged "peremptorily" without giving a reason, or for cause. Holinshed's account makes no mention of the fact that Throckmorton himself challenged *ten* of the jurors, which suggests that he had received secret information about their dispositions. See Bellamy, *Tudor Law of Treason*, 140, and his citation of *Public Record Office*, KB 8/29 m.10. The chief irony, however, was that the Crown's challenges resulted in the appointment of the two most intransigent jurors, Thomas Whetston, haberdasher, who became foreman, and Emanuel Lucar, merchant-tailor.

[8] Perhaps a reference to Mary's replacement of Cholmley, as chief justice of king's bench, by Sir Thomas Bromley.

[Throckmorton]: Ah, ah, Master Cholmley, will this foul packing never be left.

Cholmley: Why, what do I, I pray you, Mr. Throckmorton? I did nothing, I am sure. You do pick quarrels to me.

Throckmorton: Well, Master Cholmley, if you do well, it is better for you, God help you.

The jury was then sworn, and proclamation made, that whosoever would give evidence against Sir Nicholas Throckmorton, knight, should come in and be heard, for the prisoner stood upon his deliverance. Whereupon sergeant Stanford presented himself to speak.

Throckmorton: And it may please you, Master Sergeant, and the others my masters of the queen's learned counsel, like as I was minded to have said a few words to the commissioners, if I might have had leave, for their better remembrance of their duties in this place of justice, and concerning direct indifferency to be used towards me this day: so by your patience I do think good to say somewhat to you, and to the rest of the queen's learned counsel, appointed to give evidence against me. And albeit you and the rest by order be appointed to give evidence against me, and entertained to set forth the depositions and matter against me; yet I pray you remember I am not alienate from you, but that I am your Christian brother; neither you so charged, but you ought to consider equity; nor yet so privileged, but that you have a duty of God appointed you how you shall do your office; which if you exceed, will be grievously required at your hands. It is lawful for you to use your gifts which I know God hath largely given you, as your learning, art, and eloquence, so as thereby you do not seduce the minds of the simple and unlearned jury, to credit matters otherwise than they be.

For, Master Sergeant, I know how, by persuasions, inforcements, presumptions, applying, implying, inferring, conjecturing, deducing of arguments, wresting and exceeding the law, the circumstances, the depositions and confessions, that unlearned men may be enchanted to think and judge those that be things indifferent, or at the worst but over-sights, to be great treasons. Such power orators have, and such ignorance the unlearned have. Almighty God by the mouth of his prophet doth conclude such advocates to be cursed, speaking these words: Cursed be he that doth his office craftily, corruptly, and maliciously.[9] And consider also, that my blood shall be required at your hands, and punished in you and yours, to the third and fourth generation.[10] Notwithstanding, you and the justices excuse always such erroneous doings, when they be after called in question, by the verdict of the twelve men. But I assure you, the purgation serveth you as it did Pilate, and you wash your hands of the bloodshed as Pilate did of Christ's.[11] And now to your matter.

Stanford: And it please you, my lords, I doubt not to prove, evidently and manifestly, that Throckmorton is wor-thily and rightly arraigned of these treasons, and that he was a principal deviser, procurer, and con-triver of the late rebellion: and that Wyatt was but his minister. Now, say you, Throckmorton, did not you send Winter to Wyatt into Kent, and did devise that the Tower of London should be taken, with

---

[9] Jeremiah 48:10: "Cursed be he that doth the work of the Lord deceitfully." Throckmorton chose to ignore the rest of the verse, however: "and cursed be he that keepeth back his sword from blood."

[10] Exodus, 34:7: "[The Lord]...will by no means clear the guilty; visiting the iniquity of the fathers upon the children, and upon the children's children, unto the third and to the fourth generation."

[11] Matthew 27:24: "When Pilate saw that he could prevail nothing,...he took water, and washed his hands before the multitude, saying, I am innocent of the blood of this just person."

other instructions concerning Wyatt's stir and rebellion?

Throckmorton:	May it please you that I shall answer particularly to the matters objected against me, in asmuch as my memory is not good,[12] and the same much decayed since my grievous imprisonment, with want of sleep, and other disquietness. I confess I did say to Winter that Wyatt was desirous to speak with him, as I understood.
Stanford:	Yea, Sir, and you devised together the taking of the Tower of London, and of the other great treasons.
Throckmorton:	No, I did not so. Prove it.
Stanford:	Yes, Sir, you met with Winter sundry times, as shall appear, and in sundry places.
Throckmorton:	That granted, proveth no such matter as is supposed in the indictment.
Winter's confession read by Stanford.	Stanford read Winter's confession, which was of this effect, that Throckmorton met with Winter one day in Tower Street, and told him that Sir Thomas Wyatt was desirous to speak with him, and Winter demanded where Wyatt was. Throckmorton answered, at his house in Kent, not far from Gillingham, as I heard say, where the ships lie. Then they parted at that time, and shortly after Throckmorton met with Winter, unto whom Winter said, "Master Wyatt doth much mislike the coming of the Spaniards into this realm, and feareth their short arrival here, in as much as he daily heareth thereof, doth see daily divers of them arrive here, scattered like soldiers; and therefore he thinketh good the Tower of London should be taken by a sleight, before the prince came, lest that piece[13] be delivered to the Spaniards." "How say you, Throckmorton, to

---

[12] This was disingenuous. Throckmorton had an astonishing memory, as later phases of the trial would reveal.

[13] Piece: a fortified place, a stronghold.

it?" Throckmorton answered, "I mislike it for diverse respects." "Even so do I," said Winter. At another time Throckmorton met the said Winter in Paul's, when he had sent one to my house, to seek me before, and he said to me, "You are admiral of the fleet that now goeth into Spaine?" I answered, "Yea." Throckmorton said, "When will your ships be ready?" I said, "Within ten days." Throckmorton said, "I understand you are appointed to conduct and carry the Lord Privy Seal[14] into Spain, and considering the danger of the Frenchman, which you say arm them to the sea apace, me think it well done, [if] you put my said lord and his train on land in the west country to avoid all dangers." Throckmorton said also, that Wyatt changed his purpose for taking the Tower of London. I said I was glad of it, and as for the Frenchmen, I care not much for them, I will so handle the matter that the queen's ships shall be (I warrant you) in safeguard. Another time I met with Master Throckmorton, when I came from the emperor's ambassadors, unto whom I declared, that the emperor had sent me a fair chain, and showed it unto Throckmorton, who said, "For this chain you have sold your country." I said, "It is neither French king nor emperor that can make me sell my country, but I will be a true Englishman." Then they parted. This is the sum of the talk betwixt Throckmorton and Winter.

Stanford: Now, my masters of the jury, you have heard my sayings confirmed with Winter's confession. How say you, Throckmorton, can you deny this? If you will, you shall have Winter justify it to your face.

Throckmorton: My lords, shall it please you that I shall answer?

Bromley: Yea, say your mind.

---

[14] John Russell, earl of Bedford, was Lord Privy Seal.

Throckmorton: I may truly deny some part of this confession, but because there is nothing material greatly, I suppose the whole be true, and what is herein deposed, sufficient to bring me within the compass of the indictment?

Stanford: It appeareth you were of counsel with Wyatt, in as much as you sent Winter down to him, who uttered unto him diverse traitorous devises.

Throckmorton: This is but conjectural; yet sith you will construe it so maliciously, I will recount how I sent Winter to Wyatt, and then I pray, you of the jury, judge better than Master Sergeant doth. I met by chance a servant of Master Wyatt's who demanded of me for Winter, and showed me that his master would gladly speak with him; and so, without any further declaration, desired me if I met Winter to tell him Master Wyatt's mind, and where he was. Thus much for the sending down of Winter.

Attorney: Yea, sir, but how say you to the taking of the Tower of London, which is treason?

Throckmorton: I answer, though Wyatt thought meet to attempt so dangerous an enterprise, and that Winter informed me of it, you cannot extend Wyatt's devises to be mine, and to bring me within the compass of treason. For what manner of reasoning or proof is this, Wyatt would have taken the Tower, *ergo* Throckmorton is a traitor. Winter doth make my purgation in his own confession, even now read as it was by Master Sergeant, though I said nothing; for Winter doth avow there, that I did much mislike it. And because you shall the better understand that I always did not allow these Master Wyatt's devises, I had these words to Winter, when he informed me of it. "I think Master Wyatt would no Englishman hurt, and this enterprise cannot be done without the hurt and slaughter of both parties. For I know him that hath the charge of the piece, and his brother, both men of good service, the one had in charge a piece of great importance, Bulloigne I mean, which was stoutly assailed, and notwithstanding he made a good account of it for his time. The like I am sure he will do by this his charge. Moreover, to account[15] the taking of the Tower, is very dangerous by the law." These were my words to Winter. And besides, it is very unlike that I of all men would confederate in such a matter against the Lieutenant of the Tower,[16] whose daughter my brother hath married, and his house and mine allied together by marriage sundry times within these few years.

Hare: But how say you to this, that Wyatt and you had conference together sundry times at Warner's house, and in other places?

Throckmorton: This is a very general charge, to have conference; but why was it not as lawful for me to confer with Wyatt as with you, or any other man? I then knew no more by Wyatt, than by any other. And to prove to talk with Wyatt was lawful and indifferent, the last day that I did talk with Wyatt, I saw my lord of Arundel, with other noble men and gentlemen, talk with him familiarly in the chamber of presence.

Hare: But they did not conspire nor talk of any stir against the Spaniards as you did pretend, and meant it against the queen, for you, Crofts, Rogers, and Warner did oftentimes devise in Warner's house about your traitorous purposes, or else what did you so often there?

Throckmorton: I confess I did mislike the queen's marriage with Spain, and also the coming of the Spaniards hither, and then methought I had reason to do so; for I did learn the reasons of my misliking of you, Master Hare, Master Southwell, and others in the parliament house. There I did see the whole consent of

---

[15] Account: probably a misprint for "attempt."
[16] The Lieutenant of the Tower: Sir John Bridges.

the realm against it; and I, a hearer, but no speaker, did learn my misliking of those matters confirmed by many sundry reasons amongst you. But as concerning any stir or uproar against the Spaniards, I never made any, neither procured any to be made. And for my resort to Master Warner's house, it was not to confer with Master Wyatt, but to show my friendship to my very good lord the marquis of Northampton, who was lodged there when he was enlarged.[17]

Stanford: Did not you, Throckmorton, tell Winter that Wyatt had changed his mind for the taking of the Tower, whereby it appeared evidently that you knew of his doings?

Throckmorton: Truly, I did not tell him so; but I care not greatly to give you that weapon to play you withall. Now let us see what you can make of it.

Stanford: Yea, Sir, that proveth that you were privy to Wyatt's mind in all his devises and treasons, and that there was sending betwixt you and Wyatt from time to time.

Throckmorton: What, Master Sergeant? Doth this prove against me, that I knew Wyatt did repent him of an evil devised enterprise? Is it to know Wyatt's repentance sin? No, it is but a venial sin[18] if it be any; it is not deadly. But where is the messenger or message that Wyatt sent to me touching his alteration? And yet it was lawful enough for me to hear from Wyatt at that time, as

---

[17] William Parr, marquess of Northampton, was arraigned with Northumberland on August 18, 1553, for supporting Lady Jane Grey. In December he was pardoned and released from the Tower, but was again arrested on suspicion of complicity with Wyatt. Northampton was again released from the Tower on March 24, 1554.

[18] Throckmorton is playing on the distinction between a venial, or minor sin, and a mortal sin that will endanger the soul—in secular terms, a pardonable offence as distinct from a capital crime.

from any other man, for any act that I knew he had done.

Dyer: And it may please you, my lords, and you my masters of the jury, to prove that Throckmorton is a principal doer in this rebellion, there is yet many other things to be declared: among other, there is Croft's confession, who saith, that he and you and your [ac]complices did many times devise about the whole matters, and he made you privy to all his determinations, and you showed him that you would go into the west country with the earl of Devon, to Sir Peter Carew, accompanied with others.

Throckmorton: Master Crofts is yet living, and is here this day. How happeneth it he is not brought face to face to justify this matter, neither hath been of all this time? Will you know the truth? Either he said not so, or he will not abide by it, but honestly hath reformed himself. And as for knowing his devises, I was so well acquainted with them, that I can name none of them, nor you neither as matter known to me.

Attorney: But why did you advise Winter to land my Lord Privy Seal in the west country?

Throckmorton: He that told you that my mind was to land him there, doth partly tell you a reason why I said so, if you would remember the one as well as the other. But because you are so forgetful, I will recite wherefore. In communication betwixt Winter and me, as he declared to me that the Spaniards provided to bring their prince hither, so the Frenchmen prepared to interrupt his arrival; for they began to arm to the sea, and had already certain ships on the west coast (as he heard). Unto whom I said, "that peradventure not only the queen's ships under his charge might be in jeopardy, but also my Lord Privy Seal, and all his train; the Frenchmen being well prepared to meet with them. And therefore for all events it were good you should put my said lord in the west country in case you espy any jeopardy." But what doth this prove to the treasons, if I were not able to give convenient reasons to my talk?

Stanford: Marry, Sir, now commeth the proofs of your treasons. You shall hear what Cuthbert Vaughan saith against you.

Vaughan's confession was read by Master Stanford.

Then Sergeant Stanford did read Vaughan's confession, tending to this effect: That Vaughan, coming out of Kent, met with Throckmorton at Warner's house, who, after he had done commendations from Wyatt to him, desired to know where Crofts was. Throckmorton answered, "Either at Arundel House where he lodgeth, or in Paul's." Then Vaughan desired to know how things went in London, saying, "Master Wyatt and we of Kent do much mislike the marriage with Spain, and the coming of the Spaniards, for diverse respects. Howbeit, if other countries[19] mislike them as Kent doth, they shall be but hardly welcome." And so they parted. Shortly after Throckmorton met with Vaughan in Paul's, unto whom Throckmorton declared with sundry circumstances that the Western men were in a readiness to come forwards, and that Sir Peter Carew had sent unto him even now, and that he had in order a good band of horsemen, and another of footmen. Then Vaughan demanded what the earl of Devonshire would do. Throckmorton answered, "He will mar all, for he will not go hence, and yet Sir Peter Carew would meet him with a band both of horsemen and footmen by the way at Andover for his safeguard, and also he should have been well accompanied from hence with other gentlemen. Yet all this will not move him to depart hence. Moreover, the said earl hath (as is said) discovered all the whole matter to the Chancellor,[20] or else it is

---

[19] "Country," in certain usages, as here, was the sixteenth-century equivalent of "county" in England today.

come out by his tailor, about the trimming of a shirt of mail, and the making of a cloak." At another time, Vaughan saith, Throckmorton showed him that he had sent a post to Sir Peter Carew, to come forward with as much speed as might be, and to bring his force with him. And also Throckmorton advised Vaughan to will Master Wyatt to come forward with his power; for now was the time, inasmuch as the Londoners would take his part if the matter were presented to them. Vaughan said also, that Throckmorton and Warner should have ridden with the said earl westward. Moreover the said Vaughan deposed, that Throckmorton showed him in talk of the earl of Pembroke, that the said earl would not fight against them, though he would not take their parts. Also Vaughan said that Throckmorton showed him that he would ride down into Berkshire to Sir Francis Englefield's house, there to meet his eldest brother,[21] to move him to take his part. And this was the sum of Cuthbert Vaughan's confession.

Stanford: How say you? Doth not here appear evident matter to prove you a principal, who not only gave order to Sir Peter Carew and his adherents for their rebellious acts in the west country, but also procured Wyatt to make his rebellion, appointing him and the others also when they should attempt their enterprise, and how they should order their doings from time to time. Besides all this evident matter, you were specially appointed to go away with the earl of Devon as one that would direct all things, and give order to all men. And therefore, Throckmorton, sith this matter is so manifest, and the evidence so apparent, I would advise you to confess your fault, and submit yourself to the queen's mercy.

---

[20] The Chancellor: Stephen Gardiner, bishop of Winchester.
[21] His eldest brother: Robert Throckmorton, whose daughter Elizabeth had married Sir Thomas Englefield. Francis was their son.

Bromley: How say you? Will you confess the matter, and it will be best for you?

Throckmorton: No, I will never accuse myself unjustly; but in as much as I come hither to be tried, I pray ye let me have the law favorably.

Attorney: It is apparent that you lay at London as a factor, to give intelligence as well to them in the west, as to Wyatt at Kent.

Throckmorton: How prove you that, or who doth accuse me but this condemned man?

Attorney: Why will you deny this matter? You shall have Vaughan justify his whole confession here before your face.

Throckmorton: It shall not need. I know his unshamefastness. He hath avowed some of this untrue talk before this time to my face, and it is not otherwise like, considering the price, but he will do the same again.

Attorney: My lord and masters, you shall have Vaughan to justify this here before you all, and confirm it with a book oath.

Throckmorton: He that hath said and lied, will not, being in this case, stick to swear and lie.

Then was Cuthbert Vaughan brought into the open court.

Sendall: How say you, Cuthbert Vaughan, is this your own confession, and will you abide by all this is here written?

Vaughan: Let me see it and I will tell you.

Then his confession was showed him.

Attorney: Because you of the jury may better credit him, I pray you, my lords, let Vaughan be sworn.

Then was Vaughan sworn on a book to say nothing but the truth.

Vaughan: It may please my lords and masters, I could have
been well content to have chose[n] seven years
imprisonment, though I had been a free man in the
law, rather than I would this day have given evidence against Sir Nicholas Throckmorton, against
whom I bear no displeasure. But sith I must needs
confess my knowledge, I confess all that is there
written is true. How say you, Master Throckmorton,
was there any displeasure between you and me, to
move me to say aught against you?

Throckmorton: None that I know. How say you, Vaughan, what
acquaintance was there between you and me, and
what letters of credit or token did you bring me from
Wyatt, or any other, to move me to trust you?

Vaughan: As for acquaintance, I knew you as I did other
gentlemen; and as for letters, I brought you none
other but commendations from Master Wyatt, as I
did to divers other of his acquaintance at London.

Throckmorton: You might as well forge the commendations as the
rest; but if you have done with Vaughan, my lords,
I pray you give me leave to answer.

Bromley: Speak and be short.[22]

Throckmorton: I speak generally to all that be here present, but
specially to you of my jury, touching the credit of
Vaughan's depositions against me, a condemned
man, and after to the matter: and note, I pray you,
the circumstances, as somewhat material to induce
the better. First, I pray you remember the small
familiarity betwixt Vaughan and me, as he hath
avowed before you, and moreover, to procure
credit at my hand, brought neither letter nor token
from Wyatt, nor from any other to me, which he also
hath confessed here; and I will suppose Vaughan to
be in as good condition as any other man here, that
is to say, an uncondemned man; yet I refer it to your

---

[22] Speak and be short: a doomed injunction!

good judgement, whether it were like that I, knowing only Vaughan's person from another man, and having none other acquaintance with him, would so frankly discover my mind to him in so dangerous a matter. How like (I say) is this, when divers of these gentlemen now in captivity, being my very familiars, could not depose any such matter against me, and nevertheless upon their examinations have said what they could? And though I be no wise man, I am not so rash as to utter to an unknown man (for so I may call him in comparison) a matter so dangerous for me to speak, and him to hear. But because my truth and his falsehood shall the better appear unto you, I will declare his inconstancy in uttering this his evidence. And for my better credit, it may please you, Master Southwell, I take you to witness, when Vaughan first justified this his unjust accusation against me before the lord Paget, the Lord Chamberlain,[23] you Master Southwell, and others, he referred the confirmation of this his surmised matter, to a letter sent from him to Sir Thomas Wyatt, which letter doth neither appear, nor any testimony of the said master Wyatt against me touching the matter: for I doubt not Sir Thomas Wyatt hath been examined of me, and hath said what he could directly or indirectly. Also Vaughan said, that young Edward Wyatt could confirm this matter, as one that knew this pretended discourse betwixt Vaughan and me, and thereupon I made suit that Edward Wyatt might either be brought face to face to me, or otherwise be examined.

Southwell: Master Throckmorton, you mistake your matter, for Vaughan said that Edward Wyatt did know some part of the matter, and also was privy of the letter that Vaughan sent Sir Thomas Wyatt.

---

[23] The Lord Chamberlain: Sir John Gage.

Throckmorton: Yea, Sir, that was Vaughan's last shift, when I charged him before the Master of the Horse and you, with his former allegations touching his witness, whom when he espied would not do so lewdly as he thought, then he used this alteration. But where be Edward Wyatt's depositions of any thing against me? Now it appeareth neither his first nor his last tale to be true. For you know, Master Bridges, and so doth my lord your brother, that I desired twice or thrice Edward Wyatt should be examined, and I am sure, and most assured he hath been willed to say what he could, and here is nothing deposed by him against me, either touching any letter or other conference. Or where is Vaughan's letter sent by Sir Thomas Wyatt concerning my talk?

But now I will speak of Vaughan's present estate in that he is a condemned man, whose testimony is nothing worth by any law. And because false witness is mentioned in the gospel, treating of accusation, hark I pray you what St. Jerome saith, expounding that place.[24] It is demanded why Christ's accusers be called false witnesses, which did report Christ's words not as he spake them. "They be false witnesses," saith St. Jerome, "which do add, alter, wrest, double, or do speak for hope to avoid death, or for malice to procure another man's death: for all men may easily gather he cannot speak truly of me, or in the case of another man's life, where he hath hope of his own by accusation."

---

[24] That place: Matthew 26:59–61: "Now the chief priests, and elders, and all the council, sought false witness against Jesus, to put him to death; But found none: yet, though many false witnesses came, yet found they none. At the last came two false witnesses. And said, This fellow said, I am able to destory the temple of God, and to build it in three days." This passage, in Throckmorton's favorite gospel, was probably important to him also because, despite the irregular circumstances of Christ's nighttime trial, even the high priests accepted the need for two witnesses.

Thus much speaketh St. Jerome[25] of false witness. By the civil law there be many exceptions to be taken against such testimonies; but because we be not governed by that law, neither have I my trial by it, it shall be superfluous to trouble you therewith, and therefore you shall hear what your own law doth say. There was a statute made in my late sovereign lord and master his time, touching accusation, and these be the words:

> *Be it enacted*, that no person nor persons, &c: shall be indicted, arraigned, condemned, or convicted for any offence of treason, petit treason, misprision of treason, for which the same offendor shall suffer any pains of death, imprisonment, loss or forfeiture of his goods, lands, &c: unless the same offender be accused by two sufficient and lawful witnesses, or shall willingly without violence confess the same.

And also in the sixth year of his reign, it is thus ratified as ensueth:

> That no person nor persons shall be indicted, arraigned, condemned, convicted or attainted of the treasons or offenses aforesaid, or for any other treasons that now be, or hereafter shall be; unless the same offender or offenders be thereof accused by two lawful and sufficient accusers, which at the time of the arraignment of the parties so accused (if they be then living) shall be brought in person before the said party accused, and avow and maintain that they have to say against the said party, to prove him guilty of the treasons or offence contained in the bill of indictment laid against the party arraigned, unless the said party arraigned shall be willing without violence to confess the same.

---

[25] St. Jerome: from his *Commentary on Matthew*, Book IV: "Sed falsus testis est qui non eodem sensu dicta intellegit quo dicuntur. Dominus enim dixerat de templo corporis sui, sed et in ipsis verbis calumniantur, et paucis additis vel mutatis." See *Patrologia Latina*, LXXVII, 259–60. Note that Throckmorton has considerably expanded St. Jerome's definition, to include the case of false witnesses who hope to spare their own life.

Here note (I pray you) that our law doth require two lawfull and sufficient accusers to be brought face to face, and Vaughan is but one, and the same most unlawful and insufficient. For who can be more unlawful and insufficient than a condemned man, and such one as knoweth to accuse me is the means to save his own life? Remember (I pray you) how long and how many times Vaughan's execution hath been respited, and how often he hath been conjured to accuse (which by God's grace he withstood until the last hour) what time perceiving there was no way to live, but to speak against me or some other (his former grace being taken away) did redeem his life most unjustly and shamefully, as you see.

Hare: Why should he accuse you more than any other, seeing there was no displeasure between you, if the matter had not been true?

Throckmorton: Because he must either speak of some man, or suffer death, and then he did rather choose to hurt him whom he least knew, and so loved least, than any other well known to him, whom he loved most. But to you of my jury I speak specially, and therefore I pray you note what I say. In a matter of less weight than trial of life and land, a man may by the law take exceptions to such as be empanelled to try the controversies betwixt the parties: as for example, a man may challenge that the sheriff is his enemy, and therefore hath made a partial return; or because one of the jury is the sheriff my adversary's servant; and also in case my adversary's villein or bondman be empanelled, I may lawfully challenge him, because the adversary part hath power over his villein's lands and goods, and hath the use of his body for servile office. Much more I may of right take exception to Vaughan's testimony, my life and all that I have depending thereupon, and the same Vaughan being more bound to the queen's highness my adversary (that woe is me therefore), but so the law doth here so term her majesty, than any villein is to his lord: for her highness hath not only power over his body, lands and goods, but over his life also.

Stanford: Yea, the exception[s] are to be taken against the jury in that case, but not against the witness or accuser, and therefore your argument serveth little for you.

Throckmorton: That is not so, for the use of the jury, and the witness and the effect of their doings doth serve me to my purpose, as the law shall discuss. And thus I make my comparison. By the civil law the judge doth give sentence upon the depositions of the witness, and by your law the judge doth give judgement upon the verdict of the jury; so as the effect is both one. To finish the matter, trial in law [is] as well by the depositions of the witness as by the jury's verdict, though they vary in form and circumstance. And so Vaughan's testimony, being credited, may be the material cause of my condemnation, as the jury to be induced by his depositions to speak their verdict, and so finally thereupon the judge to give sentence. Therefore I may use the same exceptions against the jury, or any of them, as the principal mean that shall occasion my condemnation.[26]

Bromley: Why, do you deny that every part of Vaughan's tale is untrue?[27]

Attorney: You may see he will deny all, and say there was no such communication betwixt them.

Throckmorton: I confess some part of Vaughan's confession to be true, as the name, the places, the time, and some part of the matter.

---

[26] This is a logical but extra-legal argument. Stanford was correct in explaining that the principle of being able to take exception against, and so remove, members of the jury on suspicion of prejudice did not and still does not apply to witnesses.

[27] An early modern double negative; we would expect, "do you deny that [it] is true?"

Attorney:	So you of the jury may perceive the prisoner doth confess some thing to be true.
Throckmorton:	As touching my sending to Sir Peter Carew, or his sending to me, or concerning my advice to Master Wyatt to stir or repair hither, or touching the earl of Devonshire parting hence, and my going with him, and also concerning the matter of the earl of Pembroke,[28] I do avow and say that Vaughan hath said untruly.
Southwell:	As for my lord of Pembroke, you need not excuse the matter, for he hath showed himself clear in these matters like a noble man, and that we all know.
Hare:	Why, what was the talk betwixt Vaughan and you so long in Paul's, if these were not so, and what meant your oft meetings?
Throckmorton:	As for our often meetings, they were of no set purpose, but by chance, and yet no oftener than twice. But sithence you would know what communication passed betixt us in Paul's, I will declare. We talked of the incommodities of the marriage of the queen with the prince of Spain, and how grievous the Spaniards would be to us here.

Vaughan said, that it should be very dangerous for any man that truly professed the gospel to live here, such was the Spaniards' cruelty, and especially against Christian men. Whereunto I answered, "It was the plague of God justly come upon us; and now almighty God dealt with us as he did with the Israelites, taking from them for their unthankfulness their godly kings, and did send tyrants to reign over them. Even so he handled us Englishmen, which had a most godly and virtuous prince to reign over us, my late sovereign lord and master, King Edward, under whom we might both safely and lawfully profess God's word, which with

---

[28] Pembroke: Sir William Herbert, first earl of Pembroke.

our lewd doings, demeanor, and living we handled so irreverently that to whip us for our faults he would send us strangers, yea, such very tyrants to exercise great tyranny over us, and did take away the virtuous and faithful king from amongst us. For every man of every estate did color his naughty affections with a pretence of religion, and made the gospel a stalking horse to bring their evil desires to effect." This was the sum of our talk in Paul's, somewhat more dilated.

Stanford: That it may appear yet more evidently how Throckmorton was a principal doer and counsellor in this matter, you shall hear his own confession of his own handwriting.

The clerk began to read, Throckmorton desired Master Stanford to read it, and the jury well to mark it. Then Master Stanford did read the prisoner's own confession to this effect:

That Throckmorton had conference with Wyatt, Carew, Crofts, Rogers and Warner, as well of the queen's marriage with the prince of Spain, as also of religion, and did particularly confer with every the forenamed of the matters aforesaid. Morever, with Sir Thomas Wyatt the prisoner talked of the bruit[29] that the western men should much mislike the coming of the Spaniards into this realm, being reported also that they intended to interrupt their arrival here. And also that it was said, that they were in consultation about the same at Exeter. Wyatt also did say, that Sir Peter Carew could not bring the same matter to good effect, nor that there was any man so meet to bring it to good effect as the earl of Devonshire,[30] and specially in the west parts,[31] insomuch as they drew not all by one line. Then

---

[29] Bruit: rumor.

[30] Edward Courtenay, earl of Devon.

[31] 1577 edition reads "West Country."

Throckmorton asked how the Kentishmen were affected to the Spaniards. Wyatt said, "The people like them evil enough, and that appeared now at the coming of the county[32] of Egmont, for they were ready to stir against him and his train, supposing it had been the prince." "But," said Wyatt, "Sir Robert Southwell, Master Baker and Master Moyle, and their affinity, which be in good credit in some places of the shire, will for other malicious respects hinder the liberty of their country." Then Throckmorton should say, "Though I know there hath been an unkindness betwixt Master Southwell and you for a money matter, wherein I travelled to make you friends, I doubt not, but in so honest a matter as this is, he will for the safeguard of his country join with you, and so you may be sure of the Lord Abergavenny and his force." Then Wyatt said, "It is for another matter than for money that we disagree, wherein he hath handled me and others very doubly and unneighborly. Howbeit, he can do no other, neither to me, nor to any other man, and therefore I forgive him." *Item,* with Sir Peter Carew Throckmorton had conference touching the impeachment of the landing of the said prince, and touching provision of armor and munition as ensueth, that is to say, that Sir Peter Carew told Throckmorton that he trusted his countrymen would be true Englishmen, and would not agree to let the Spaniards to govern them. *Item,* the said Sir Peter Carew said, the matter importing the French king as it did, he thought the French king would work to hinder the Spaniards coming hither, which whom the said Sir Peter did think good to practise for armor, munition, and money.

Then Throckmorton did advise him to beware that he brought any Frenchmen into the realm forcibly, inasmuch as he could as evil abide the

---

[32] County: count.

Frenchmen after that sort as the Spaniards. And also Throckmorton thought the French king unable to give aid to us, by means of the great consumption in their own wars. Master Carew said, as touching the bringing in of the Frenchmen, he meant it not, for he loved neither party, but to serve his own country, and to help his country from bondage; declaring further to Throckmorton, that he had a small bark of his own to work his practise by, and so he said, that shortly he intended to depart to his own country, to understand the devotion of his countrymen.[33] *Item*, Throckmorton did say, he would for his part hinder the coming in of the Spaniards as much as he could by persuasion.[34] *Item*, to Sir Edward Warner, he had and did bemoan his own estate, and the tyranny of the time extended upon divers honest persons for religion, and wished it were lawful for all of each religion to live safely according to their conscience.[35] For the law *ex officio*[36] will be intolerable, and the clergy's discipline now may rather be resembled to the Turks' tyranny than to the teaching of christian religion.

This was the sum of the matter which was read in the foresaid confession, as matters most grievous against the prisoner. Then Throckmorton said:

Throckmorton: Sithence, Master Sergeant, you have read and gathered the place (as you think) that maketh most against me, I pray you, take the pains and read further, that hereafter whatsoever become of me, my words be not perverted and abused to the hurt

---

[33] In this sentence, "country" twice refers to England as a whole, and then switches to Carew's county, Devon.

[34] By persuasion: this is a crucial aspect of Throckmorton's defence—that he had expressed his antagonism to the queen's policy by words alone.

[35] For all of each religion to live safely according to their conscience: a remarkable early expression of religious toleration.

[36] See Introduction, n.17.

of some others, and especially against the great personages, of whom I have been sundry times (as appeareth by my answers) examined, for I perceive the net was not cast only for little fishes, but for the great ones, *iuxta adagium.*[37]

Sanford: It shall be but loss of time, and we have other things to charge you withall, and this that you desire doth make nothing for you.

Dyer: And for the better confirmation of all the treasons objected against the prisoner, and therein to prove him guilty, you of the jury shall hear the duke of Suffolk's depositions against him, who was a principal, and hath suffered accordingly.

Then the said sergeant read the duke's confession touching the prisoner, amounting to this effect, that the lord Thomas Grey did inform the said duke, that Sir Nicholas Throckmorton was privy to the whole devises against the Spaniards, and was one that should go into the west country with the earl of Devonshire.

Throckmorton: But what doth the principal author of this matter say against me, I mean the lord Thomas Grey who is yet living? Why be not his depositions brought against me, for so it ought to be, if he can say any thing? Will you know the truth? Neither the lord Thomas Grey hath said, can say, or will say anything against me, notwithstanding the duke his brother's confession and accusation, who hath affirmed many other things besides the truth. I speak not without certain knowledge: for the lord Thomas Grey, being my prison-fellow for a small time, informed me that the duke his brother had misreported him in many things, amongst others in matters touching me, which he had declared to you, Master Southwell, and others the examiners, not long ago. I am sure if the lord Thomas could or would have said anything, it should have been here now. And as to the

---

[37] *Juxta adagium*: as in the proverb.

duke's confession, it is not material; for he doth refer the matter to the lord Thomas's report, who hath made my purgation.

Attorney: And it please you, my lords and you my masters of the jury, besides these matters touching Wyatt's rebellion, Sir Peter Carew's treasons and confederating with the duke of Suffolk, and besides the prisoner's conspiracy with the earl of Devonshire, with Crofts, Rogers, Warner, and sundry others in sundry places, it shall manifestly appear unto you, that Throckmorton did conspire the queen's majesty's death with William Thomas, Sir Nicholas Arnold, and other traitors intending the same, which is the greatest matter of all others, and most to be abhorred. And for proof hereof, you shall hear what Arnold saith.

Then was Sir Nicholas Arnold's confession read, saying that Throckmorton showed to him, riding betwixt Hinam and Crossland in Gloucestershire, that John Fitzwilliams was very much displeased with William Thomas.

Attorney: William Thomas devised, that John Fitzwilliams should kill the queen, and Throckmorton knew of it, as appeareth by Arnold's confession.

Throckmorton: First, I deny that I said any such thing to Master Arnold, and though he be an honest man, he may either forget himself, or devise means how to unburden himself of so weighty a matter as this is; for he is charged with the matter as principal. Which I did perceive when he charged me with his tale, and therefore I do blame him the less, that he seeketh how to discharge himself using me as a witness, if he could so transfer the devise to William Thomas. But truly I never spake any such words unto him. And for my better declaration, I did see John Fitzwilliams here even now, who can testify that he never showed me of any displeasure betwixt them, and as I know nothing of the displeasure betwixt them, so I know nothing of the cause. I pray you, my lords, let him be called to depose in this matter what he can.

Then John Fitzwilliams drew to the bar, and presented himself to depose his knowledge in the matter in open court.

Attorney: I pray you, my lords, suffer him not to be sworn, neither to speak; we have nothing to do with him.

Throckmorton: Why should he not be suffered to tell truth? And why be ye not so well contented to hear truth for me as untruth against me?

Hare: Who called you hither, Fitzwilliams, or commanded you to speak? You are a very busy officer.

Throckmorton: I called him, and do humbly desire that he may speak, and be heard as well as Vaughan; or else I am not indifferently used, especially seeing Master Attorney doth so press this matter against me.

Southwell: Go your ways, Fitzwilliams, the court hath nothing to do with you. Peradventure you would not be so ready in a good cause.

Then John Fitzwilliams departed the court, and was not suffered to speak.

Throckmorton: Sithence this gentleman's declaration may not be admitted, I trust you of the jury can perceive it was not for anything he had to say against me, but contrariwise that it was feared he would speak for me. And now to Master Arnold's depositions against me, I say I did not tell him any such words; so as if it were material, there is but his yea and my nay. But because[38] the words be not forestrained against me, I pray you, Master Attorney, why might not I have told Master Arnold that John Fitzwilliams was angry with William Thomas, and yet know no cause of the anger? It might be understand, to disagree oftentimes.[39] Who doth confess that I know anything of

---

[38] Because...not: i.e. lest.

William Thomas's devise touching the queen's death? I will answer, no man. For Master Arnold doth mention no word of that matter, but of the displeasures betwixt them. And to speak that, doth neither prove treason, nor knowledge of treason. Is here all the evidence against me that you have to bring me within the compass of the indictment?

Stanford: Methinks the matters confessed by others against you, together with your own confession, will weigh shrewdly. But how say you to the rising in Kent, and to Wyatt's attempt against the queen's royal person at her palace?

Bromley: Why do you not read Wyatt's accusation to him, which doth make him partner to his treasons?

Southwell: Wyatt hath grievously accused you, and in many things that others have confirmed.

Throckmorton: Whatsoever Wyatt hath said of me in hope of his life, he unsaid it at his death. For since I came into this hall, I heard one say (but I know him not) that Wyatt upon the scaffold did not only purge my Lady Elizabeth her grace, and the earl of Devonshire, but also all the gentlemen in the Tower, saying they were all ignorant of the stir and commotion. In which number I take myself.

Hare: Notwithstanding, he said all that he had written and confessed to the Council was true.

Throckmorton: Nay, sir, by your patience, Master Wyatt said not so, that was Master Doctor's addition.[40]

Southwell: It appeareth you have had good intelligence.

Throckmorton: Almighty God provided that revelation for me this day since I came hither; for I have been in close

---

[39] This is the only unintelligible place in the text. A possible reading: "They might be understood to disagree oftentimes."

[40] Master Doctor: Dr. Hugh Weston, the clergyman who attended Wyatt at his execution.

prison these eight and fifty days, where I heard nothing but what the birds told me, which did fly over my head.[41] And now to you of my jury I speak specially, whom I desire to mark attentively what shall be said. I have been indicted, as it appeareth, and now am arraigned of compassing the queen's majesty's death, of levying war against the queen, of taking the Tower of London, of deposing and depriving the queen of her royal estate, and finally to destroy her, and of adherence to the queen's enemies. Of all which treasons, to prove me guilty, the queen's learned counsel hath given in evidence these points material: that is to say, for the compassing or imagining the queen's death, and the destruction of her royal person, Sir Nicholas Arnold's depositions, which is that I should say to the said Sir Nicholas in Gloucestershire, that Master John Fitzwilliams was angry with William Thomas.

Whereunto I have answered as you have heard, both denying the matter; and for the proof on my side, do take exceptions, because there is no witness but one. And nevertheless, though it were granted, the depositions prove nothing concerning the queen's death. For levying of war against the queen, there is alleged my conference with Sir Thomas Wyatt, Sir James Crofts, Sir Edward Rogers, Sir Edward Warner. Against the marriage with Spain, and the coming of the Spaniards hither, which talk I do not deny in sort as I spake it, and meant it; and notwithstanding the malicious gathering this day of my conference, proveth yet no levying of war. There is also alleged for proof of the same article, Sir James Croft's confession, which (as you remember) implieth no such thing, but general talk against the marriage with Spain. And of my

---

[41] This is also clearly disingenuous. See *The Legend of Sir Nicholas Throckmorton*, in Appendix A, Stanza 129, where it is implied that someone smuggled law books into the Tower.

departing westward with the earl of Devon, which the said Sir James doth not avow, and therefore I pray you consider it as not spoken. There is also for proof of the said article, the duke of Suffolk's confession, which whom I never had conference, and therefore he avouched the tale of his brother's mouth, who hath made my purgation in those matters; and yet if the matter were proved, they be not greatly material in law. There is also alleged for the further proof of the same article, and for deposing and depriving the queen of her royal estate, and for my adhering to the queen's enemies, Cuthbert Vaughan's confession, whose testimony I have sufficiently disproved by sundry authorities and circumstances, and principally by your own law, which doth require two lawful and sufficient witnesses to be brought face to face. Also for the taking of the Tower of London, there is alleged Winter's depositions, which uttereth my misliking, when he uttered unto me Sir Thomas Wyatt's resolution and devise for attempting of the said piece. And last of all, to enforce these matters, mine own confession is engrieved[42] against me, wherein there doth appear neither treason, neither concealment of treason, neither whispering of treason, nor procurement of treason.

And forsomuch as am I come hither to be tried by the law, though my innocency of all these points material objected be apparent to acquit me, whereto I do principally cleave; yet I will for your better credit and satisfactions show you evidently, that if you would believe all the depositions laid against me, which I trust you will not do, I ought not to be attainted of the treason comprised within my indictment, considering the statute of repeal the last parliament, of all treasons other than such as be declared in the five and twentieth year of King Edward the

---

[42] Engrieved: made a grievance of.

	third, both which statutes, I pray you, my lords, may be read here to the inquest.
Bromley:	No, Sir, there shall be no books brought at your desire. We do all know the law sufficiently without book.
Throckmorton:	Do you bring me hither to try me by the law, and will not show me the law? What is your knowledge of the law to these men's satisfactions, which have my trial in hand? I pray you, my lords, and my lords all, let the statutes be read, as well for the queen, as for me.
Stanford:	My Lord Chief Justice can show the law, and will, if the jury do doubt of any point.
Throckmorton:	You know it were indifferent that I should know and hear the law whereby I am adjudged, and forasmuch as the statute is in English, men of meaner learning than the justices can understand it, or else how should we know when we offend?
Hare:	You know not what belongeth to your case, and therefore we must teach you. It appertaineth not to us to provide books for you, neither sit we here to be taught of you. You should have taken better heed to the law before you had come hither.
Throckmorton:	Because I am ignorant, I would learn, and therefore I have more need to see the law, and partly as well for the instructions of the jury, as for my own satisfaction, which me think were for the honor of this presence. And now if it please you, my Lord Chief Justice, I do direct my speech specially to you. What time it pleased the queen's majesty to call you to this honorable office, I did learn of a great personage of her highness's Privy Council that, amongst other good instructions, her majesty charged and enjoined you to minister the law and justice indifferently without respect of persons. And notwithstanding the old error[43] amongst you, which did not

---

[43] The old error: Throckmorton thus cheekily designates the legal principle

admit any witness to speak or any other matter to be heard in the favor of the adversary, her majesty being party, her highness's pleasure was that whatsoever could be brought in the favor of the subject should be admitted to be heard. And, moreover, that you specially, and likewise all other justices, should not persuade themselves to sit in judgement otherwise for her highness than for her subject. Therefore this manner of indifferent proceeding being principally enjoined by God's commandment, which I had thought partly to have remembered you and others here in commission, in the beginning, if I might have had leave, and the same also being commanded you by the queen's own mouth; me think you ought of right to suffer me to have the statutes read openly, and also to reject nothing that could be spoken in my defence; and in thus doing, you shall show yourselves worthy ministers, and fit for so worthy a mistress.

Bromley: You mistake the matter. The queen spake those words to Master Morgan,[44] Chief Justice of the Common Pleas. But you have no cause to complain, for you have been suffered to talk at your pleasure.

Hare: What would you do with the statute book? The jury doth not require it. They have heard the evidence, and they must upon their conscience try whether you be guilty or no, so as the book needeth not. If they will not credit the evidence so apparent, then they know not what they have to do.

Cholmley: You ought not to have any books read here at your appointment, for where doth arise any doubt in the law, the judges sit here to inform the court, and now you do but spend time.

---

that in a treason trial anyone defending the accused will be deemed to speak against the monarch.

[44] Morgan: Sir Richard Morgan.

Attorney:	I pray you, my Lord Chief Justice, repeat the evidence for the queen, and give the jury their charge, for the prisoner will keep you here all day.
Bromley:	How say you? Have you any more to say for yourself?[45]
Throckmorton:	You seem to give and offer me the law, but in very deed I have only the form and image of the law. Nevertheless, sith I cannot be suffered to have the statutes read openly in the book, I will by your patience guess at them as I may, and I pray you to help me if I mistake, for it is long since I did see them. The statute of repeal made the last parliament hath these words:

> Be it enacted by the Queen, that from henceforth none act, deed, or offence, being by act of parliament or statute made treason, petit treason, or misprision of treason, by words, writing, printing, ciphering, deeds, or otherwise whatsoever, shall be taken, had, deemed, or adjudged treason, petit treason, but only such as be declared or expressed to be treason, in or by an act of parliament made in the five and twentieth year of Edward the third, touching and concerning treasons, and the declaration of treasons, and none other.

Here may you see, this statute doth refer all the offences aforesaid to the statute of the five and twentieth year of Edward the third, which statute hath these words touching and concerning the treasons that I am indicted and arraigned of, that is to say:

> Whosoever doth compass or imagine the death of the king, or levy war against the king in his realm, or being adherent to the king's enemies within this realm or elsewhere, and be thereof probably attainted by open deed[46] by people of their condition, shall be adjudged a traitor.

---

[45] Have you any more to say for yourself?: another fatal mistake on Bromley's part.

[46] By open deed: The statute quoted (25 Edward III. 5. cap. 2) reads "of open

Now, I pray you of my jury which have my life in trial, note well what things at this day be treasons, and how these treasons must be tried and discerned; that is to say, by open deed, which the laws doth at some time term "*overt act*".[47] And now I ask notwithstanding my indictment, which is but matter alleged, where doth appear the open deed of any compassing or imagining the queen's death? Or where doth appear any open deed of being adherent to the queen's enemies, giving to them aid and comfort? Or where doth appear any open deed of taking the Tower of London?

Bromley: Why do not you of the queen's learned counsel answer him? Me think, Throckmorton, you need not have the statutes, for you have them meetly, perfectly.

Stanford: You are deceived to conclude all treasons in the statute of the five and twentieth year of Edward the third; for that statute is but a declaration of certain treasons, which were treasons before at the common law. Even so there doth remain divers other treasons at this day in the common law, which be expressed by that statute, as the judges can declare. Nevertheless, there is matter sufficient alleged and proved against you, to bring you within the compass of the same statute.

Throckmorton: I pray you, express those matters that bring me within the compass of the statute of Edward the third. For the words be these: "And be thereof attainted by open deed, by people of like condition."

Bromley: Throckmorton, you deceive yourself, and mistake these words, "By people of their condition." For thereby the law doth understand the discovering of

---

deed," which makes considerable difference to the sense.

[47] This phrase is highlighted in the 1577 text not only by parentheses, but also by being set in a Roman type.

your treasons. As, for example, Wyatt and the other rebels, attainted for their great treasons, already declare you to be his and their adherent, inasmuch as divers and sundry times you had conference with him and them about the treason, so as Wyatt is now one of your condition, who (all the world knoweth) hath committed an open traitorous fact.

Throckmorton: By your leave, my lord, this is a very strange and singular understanding. For I suppose the meaning of the law-makers did understand these words, "By people of their condition," of the state and condition of those persons which should be on the inquest to try the party arraigned,[48] guilty or not guilty, and nothing to the betraying of the offence by another man's act, as you say. For what have I do do with Wyatt's acts, that was not nigh him by one hundred miles?

Attorney: Will you take upon you to skill better of the law than the judges? I doubt not but you of the jury will credit as it becometh you.

Cholmley: Concerning the true understanding of these words, "By people of their condition," my lord Chief Justice here hath declared the truth, for Wyatt was one of your condition, that is to say, of your conspiracy.

Hare: You do not deny, Throckmorton, but that there hath been conference and sending between Wyatt and you; and he and Winter doth confess the same, with others, so as it is plain, Wyatt may be called one of your condition.

Throckmorton: Well, seeing you my judges rule the understanding of these words in the statute, "By people of your condition," thus strangely against me, I will not stand longer upon them. But where doth appear in me an

---

[48] Throckmorton was quite correct in his understanding. The Edwardian statute referred to the principle of the right to be tried by a jury of one's peers.

open deed whereunto the treason is specially referred?

Bromley: If three or four do talk, devise and conspire together of a traitorous act to be done, and afterwards one of them doth commit treason, as Wyatt did, then the law doth repute them, and every of them as their acts, so as Wyatt's act do imply and argue of your open deed: and so the law doth term it and take it.

Throckmorton: These be marvellous expositions and wonderful implications, that another man's act, whereof I was not privy, should be accounted mine; for Wyatt did purge me that I knew nothing of his stir.

Hare: Yea, Sir, but you were a principal procurer and contriver of Wyatt's rebellion, though you were not with him when he made the stir. And as my lord here hath said, the law always doth adjudge him a traitor which was privy and doth procure treason, or any other man to commit treason or a traitorous act, as you did Wyatt and others; for so the *overt act* of those which did it by your procurement shall in this case be accounted your open deed. We have a common case in the law, if one by procurement should disseize you of your land, the law holdeth us both wrongdoers, and giveth remedy against the one as the other.

Throckmorton: For God's sake, apply not such constructions against me, and though my present estate doth not move you, yet it were well you should consider your office, and think what measure you give to others, you yourselves, I say, shall assuredly receive the same again.[49] The state of mortal life is such, that men know full little what hangeth over them. I put on within these twelve months such a mind, that I,

[49] See Matthew 7:2: "With what measure ye mete, it shall be measured to you again"; and compare also Shakespeare's *Measure for Measure*, a play about the maladministration of justice that expounds on this text.

most woeful wight, was as unlike to stand here, as some of you that sit there. As to your case last recited, whereby you would conclude; I have remembered, and learned of you, Master Hare and you Master Stanford, in the parliament house, where you did sit to make laws, to expound and explain the ambiguities and doubts of law sincerely, and that without affections.[50] There, I say, I learned of you, and others my masters of the law, this difference betwixt such cases as you remembered one even now, and the statute whereby I am to be tried. There is a maxim or principle in the law, which ought not to be violated, that no penal statute may, ought, or should be construed, expounded, extended, or wrested, otherwise than the simple words and nude letter of the same statute doth warrant and signify. And amongst divers good and notable reasons by you there in the parliament house debated (Master Sergeant Stanford) I noted this one, why the said maxim ought to be inviolable. You said, considering the private affections many times both of princes and ministers within this realm, for that they were men and could and would err, it should be no security, but very dangerous to the subject, to refer the construction and extending of penal statutes to any judge's equity (as you termed it), which might either by fear of the higher powers be seduced, or by ignorance and folly abused.[51] And that is an answer by procurement.

---

[50] An allusion to the venerable definition of law as "mens sine affectu," originating in Aristotle's *Politics*, 3:11:4–5.

[51] This passage is somewhat abstruse. It refers to the sixteenth-century extension of the legal concept of *equity*, that which softens the rigors of strict law, into the realm of the *interpretation* of statutes. This extension was a matter of legal debate, since there was some anxiety that if judges starting interpreting statutes according to their own conscience, the practice of the law might become more arbitrary and more, not less severe. See the mid-century *Discourse upon the Exposicion & Understanding of Statutes*, ed. Samuel E. Thorne (San Marino: Huntington Library, 1942), esp. page 3.

Bromley: Nothwithstanding the principle (as you allege it) and the preciseness of your sticking to the bare words of the statute, it doth appear and remain of record in our learning, that divers cases have been adjudged treason without the express words of the statute, as the queen's learned counsel there can declare.

Attorney: It doth appear the prisoner did not only entice or procure Wyatt, Carew, Rogers and others to commit their traitorous act, and there doth his open facts appear, which Vaughan's confession doth witness, but also he did mind shortly after to associate himself with those traitors; for he minded to have departed with the earl of Devonshire westward.

Throckmorton: My innocency concerning these matters I trust sufficiently appeareth by my former answers, notwithstanding the condemned man's unjust accusation. But because the true understanding of the statute is in question, I say procurement, and specially by words only, is without the compass of it, and that I do learn and prove by the principle which I learned of Master Stanford.

Stanford: Master Throckmorton, you and I may not agree this day in the understanding of the law, for I am for the queen, and you are for yourself.[52] The judges must determine the matter.

Bromley: He that doth procure another man to commit a felony or murder, I am sure you know well enough, the law doth adjudge the procurer there a felon or a murderer; and in case of treason it hath been always so taken and reputed.

Throckmorton: I do and must cleave to my innocency, for I procured no man to commit treason; but yet for my learning I desire to hear some case so ruled when the law was as it is now. I do confess it, that at such

---

[52] 1577 reads: "You speak for yourself."

Happy for
Throckmorton
that those
the statutes
stood then
repealed

time there were statutes provided for the procurer, counsellor, aider, abettor, and such like, as there were in King Henry the eighth's time. You might lawfully make this cruel construction, and bring the procurer within the compass of the law. But these statutes being repealed, you ought not now so to do; and as to the principal procurer in felony or murder, it is like as in treason; for the principal and accessories in felony and murder be triable and punishable by the common law, and so in those cases the judges may use their equity, extending the determination of the fault as they think good. But in treason it is otherwise, the same being limited by statute, which I say and avow is restrained from any judge's construction, by the maxim that I recited.

Stanford: Your lordships do know a case in Richard the third's time, where the procurer to counterfeit false money was judged a traitor, and the law was as it is now.

Hare: Master Sergeant doth remember you, Throckmorton, of an experience before our time, that the law hath been so taken; and yet the procurer was not expressed in the statute, but the law hath been always so taken.

Throckmorton: I never studied the law, whereof I do much repent me; yet I remember, whilst penal statutes were talked of in the parliament house, you the learned men of the house remembered some cases contrary to this last spoken of. And if I misreport them, I pray you help me. In the like case you speak of concerning the procurer to counterfeit false money, at one time the procurer was judged a felon, and at another time neither felon nor traitor. So as some of your predecessors adjudged the procurer no traitor in the same case, but leaned to their principle, though some other extend their constructions too large. And here is two cases with me, for one against me.

Bromley: Because you rely upon the principle, I will remember where one taking the great seal of England from one writing and putting it to another was adjudged a traitor in Henry the fourth's time, and yet his act was not within the express words of the statute of Edward the third. There be divers other such like cases that may be alleged, and need were.

Throckmorton: I pray you, my lord Chief Justice, call to your good remembrance that in the self same case of the seal, Justice Spelman, a grave and well learned man, since that time would not condemn the offender, but did reprove that former judgement by you last remembered as erroneous.[53]

Stanford: If I thought you had been so well furnished in book cases, I would have been better provided for you.

Throckmorton: I have nothing but I learned of you specially, Master Sergeant, and of others my masters of the law in the parliament house, and therefore I may say with the prophet *Salutem ex inimicis nostris.*[54]

Southwell: You have a very good memory.

Attorney: If the prisoner may avoid his treasons after this manner, the queen's surety shall be in great jeopardy. For Jack Cade,[55] the blacksmith,[56] and divers

---

[53] For the case, see *Year Books*, 2 Henry IV, Trin. pl. 25. And see John Bellamy, *The Law of Treason in the later Middle Ages* (Cambridge: Cambridge University Press, 1970), 134. Bellamy states that the case "seemed to the Tudor lawyers to lie outside the statute," but does not cite Spelman, whose opinion I have been unable to find.

[54] Luke 1:71, from the Vulgate version of the prophecy of Zacharias, which Throckmorton would soon quote more fully and in English.

[55] Jack Cade: Calling himself Mortimer, he led a rebellion against Henry VI in 1450.

[56] The Blacksmith: This unnamed figure participated in the 1496 rebellion against Henry VII. His story, along with that of Jack Cade, is included in *The Mirror for Magistrates*, the generic model for *the Legend of Sir Nicholas Throckmorton*. Cade's "tragedy" was first published in the 1559 edition, that of the Blacksmith concluded the 1563 edition; but the editorial note to the reader that followed it was evidently written during Mary's reign, since it contains a defence of her succession and marriage: "The frantic heads which disable our

other traitors, sometime alleging the law for them, sometime they meant no harm to the king, but against his counsel, as Wyatt, the duke of Suffolk, and these did against the Spaniards, when there was no Spaniards within the realm. The duke and his brethren did mistake the law, as you do; yet at length did confess their ignorance, and submitted themselves. And so were you best to do.

Throckmorton: As to Cade and the blacksmith, I am not so well acquainted with their treasons as you be; but I have read in the chronicle,[57] they were in the field with a force against the prince, whereby a manifest act did appear. As to the duke of Suffolk's doings, they appertain not to me. And though you would compare my speech and talk against the Spaniards to the duke's acts, who assembled a force in arms, it is evident they differ much. I am sorry to engrieve[58] any other man's doings, but it serveth me for a piece of my defence, and therefore I wish that no man should gather evil of it. God forbid that words and acts be thus confounded.

Attorney: Sir William Stanley used this shift that the prisoner useth now. He said he did not levy war against King Henry the seventh, but said to the duke of Buckingham that in a good quarrel he would aid him with five hundred men; and nevertheless Stanley was for those words attainted, who (as all the world knoweth) had before that time served the king very faithfully and truly.

Queen, because she is a woman, and our king, because he is a stranger, to be our princes and chief governors, hath caused me to say thus much." See *The Mirror for Magistrates*, ed. L.B. Campbell (Cambridge: Cambridge University Press, 1938), 420.

[57] In the chronicle: probably Edward Hall's *The Union of the two noble and illustrious families of Lancaster & York*, published in 1548 and banned by Queen Mary in June 1555.

[58] engrieve: make a grievance of.

Throckmorton:	I pray you, Master Attorney, do not conclude against me by blind contraries. Whether you allege Stanley's case truly or no, I know not. But admit it be as you say, what doth this prove against me? I promised no aid to Master Wyatt nor to any other. The duke of Buckingham levied war against the king, with whom Stanley was confederate so to do as you say.
Attorney:	I pray you, my lords that be the queen's commissioners, suffer not the prisoner to use the queen's learned counsel thus. I was never interrupted thus in my life, nor I never knew any thus suffered to talk as this prisoner is suffered. Some of us will come no more at the bar and we be thus handled.
Bromley:	Throckmorton, you must suffer the queen's learned counsel to speak, or else we must take order with you. You have had leave to talk at your pleasure.
Hare:	It is proved that you did talk with Wyatt against the coming of the Spaniards, and devised to interrupt their arrival; and you promised to do what you could against them; whereupon Wyatt being encouraged by you, did levy a force, and attempted war against the queen's royal person.
Throckmorton:	It was no treason nor no procurement of treason to talk against the coming hither of the Spaniards, neither was it treason for me to say I would hinder their coming hither as much as I could (understanding me rightly as I mean it).[59] Yea, though you would extend it to the worst, it was but words, it was not treason at this day as the law standeth. And as for Wyatt's doing[s], they touch me nothing; for at his death, when it was no time to report untruly, he purged me.
Bromley:	But sundry cases remembered here by the queen's learned counsel (as you have heard) that procurement which did appear none otherwise but by

---

[59] i.e. by persuasion.

words—and those you would make nothing—hath been of long time, and by sundry well learned men in the laws, adjudged treason. And therefore, your procurement being so evident as it is, we may lawfully say it was treason, because Wyatt performed a traitorous act.

Throckmorton: As to the said alleged foreprecedents against me, I have recited as many for me, and I would you, my lord Chief Justice, should incline your judgements rather after the example of your honorable predecessors, Justice Markham[60] and others, which did eschew corrupt judgements, judging directly and sincerely, after the law and the principles in the same, than after such men as swerving from the truth, the maxim, and the law, did judge corruptly, maliciously, and affectionately.

Bromley: Justice Markham had reason to warrant his doings; for it did appear, a merchant of London was arraigned and slanderously accused of treason for compassing and imagining the king's death. He did say he would make his son heir of the crown, and the merchant meant it of a house in Cheapside at the sign of the Crown, but your case is not so.

Throckmorton: My case doth differ, I grant, but specially because I have not such a judge. Yet there is another cause to restrain these your strange and extraordinary con-

---

[60] Justice Markham: Chief Justice John Markham. In 1468, in the case of Sir Thomas Cook, Markham declared that what Edward IV thought was treason was misprision only. See Bellamy, *The Law of Treason in England in the later Middle Ages*, 168. Note, however, that Bromley in his reply calmly attaches Markham's statement to a case more trivial than Cook's. This became a famous anecdote in liberal legal thought. In 1581, Cardinal William Allen described how, at the trial of Edmund Campion for treason under Elizabeth, some of the audience had come "to behold whether the old honor, law and justice wherein our nation hath of all the world had the praise, could or durst stand, notwithstanding any violent impression of power and authority to the contrary: whether there were any Markhams left in the land... See See Allen, *A brief historie of the glorious martyrdom of xii reverend priests*, ed. J.H. Pollen (London, 1908), 18–19.

structions; that is to say, a proviso in the latter end of the statute of Edward the third, having these words:

> Provided always, if any other case of supposed treason shall chance hereafter to come in question or trial before any justice, other than is in the said statute expressed, that then the justice shall forbeare to adjudge the said case, until it be showed to the parliament to try whether it should be treason or felony.

Here you are restrained by express words to adjudge any case that is not manifestly mentioned before and until it be showed to the parliament.

Portman: That proviso is understood of cases that may come in trial which hath [not] been in ure,[61] but the law hath always taken the procurer to be a principal offender.

Sanders: The law always in cases of treason doth account all principals and no accessories as in other offences; and therefore a man offending in treason, either by covert act or procurement, whereupon an open deed hath ensued, as in this case, is adjudged by the law a principal traitor.

Throckmorton: You adjudge (me think) procurement very hardly, besides the principle, and besides the good proviso, and besides the good example of your best and most godly learned predecessors, the judges of the realm, as I have partly declared. And not withstanding this grievous racking and extending of this word "procurement," I am not in the danger of it, for it doth appear by no deposition that I procured neither one or other to attempt any act.

Stanford: The jury have to try whether it be so or no. Let it weigh as it will.

---

[61] Not . . . in ure: not in use, i.e. unprecedented.

Hare: I know no mean so apparent to try procurement as by words, and that mean is probable enough against you, as well by your own confession as by other men's depositions.

Throckmorton: To talk of the queen's marriage with the prince of Spain, and also the coming hither of the Spaniards, is not to procure treason to be done; for then the whole parliament house, I mean the Common[s] house, did procure treason. But sith you will make no difference betwixt words and acts, I pray you remember a statute made in my late sovereign lord and master's time, king Edward the sixth, which apparently expressed the difference. These be the words:

> Whosoever doth compass or imagine to depose the king of his royal estate by open preaching, express words or sayings, shall for the first offence lose and forfeit to the king all his and their goods and chattels, and also shall suffer imprisonment of their bodies at the king's will and pleasure. Whosoever, &c: for the second offence shall lose and forfeit to the king the whole issues and profits of all his or their lands, tenements and other hereditaments, benefices, prebends, and other spiritual promotions. Whosoever, &c: for the third offence, shall for term of life or lives of such offender or offenders, &c: and shall also forfeit to the king's majesty all his or their goods and chattels, and suffer during his or their lives perpetual imprisonment of his or their bodies. But whosoever, &c: by writing, ciphering, or act, &c: shall for the first offence be adjudged a traitor, and suffer the pains of death.

Here you may perceive how the whole realm and all your judgements before this understood words and acts diversely and apparently. And therefore the judgements of the parliament did assign diversity of punishments, because they would not confound the true understanding of words and deeds, appointing for compassing and imagining by word, imprisonment; and for compassing and imagining by open deed, pains of death.

Bromley: It is agreed by the whole Bench, that the procurer and the adherent be deemed always traitors, when as a traitorous act was committed by any one of the same conspiracy; and there is apparent proof of your adhering to Wyatt, both by your own confesson and other ways.

Throckmorton: Adhering and procuring be not all one, for the statute of Edward the third doth speak of adhering, but not of procuring; and yet adhering ought not to be further extended than to the queen's enemies within her realm, for so the statute doth limit the understanding. And Wyatt was not the queen's enemy, for he was not so reputed when I talked with him last, and our speech implied no enemy, neither tended to any treason, or procuring of treason. And therefore, I pray you of the jury note, though I argue the law, I allege mine innocency as the best part of my defence.

Hare: Your adhering to the queen's enemies within the realm is evidently proved; for Wyatt was the queen's enemy within the realm, as the whole realm knoweth it, and he hath confessed it both at his arraignment and at his death.

Throckmorton: By your leave, neither Wyatt at his arraignment nor at his death did confess that he was the queen's enemy when I last talked with him; neither was he reputed nor taken in fourteen days after, until he assembled a force in arms, what time I was at your house, Master Englefield, where I learned the first intelligence of Wyatt's stir. And, I ask you, who doth depose that there passed any manner of advertisement betwixt Wyatt and me, after he had discovered his doings, and showed himself an enemy?

If I had been so disposed, who did let me that I did not repair to Wyatt, or to send to him, or to the duke of Suffolk either, who was in my own

	country, and thither I might have gone and conveyed myself with him, unsuspected for my departing homewards?
Englefield:	It is true that you were there at my house, accompanied with others your brethren, and, to my knowledge, ignorant of these matters.
Bromley:	Throckmorton, you confessed you talked with Wyatt and others against the coming of the Spaniards, and of the taking of the Tower of London, whereupon Wyatt levied a force of men against the Spaniards he said, and so you say all; but indeed it was against the queen, which he confessed at length. Therefore Wyatt's acts do prove you counsellor and procurer, howsoever you would avoid the matter.
Throckmorton:	Methink you would conclude against me with a misshapen argument in logic; and you will give me leave, I will make another.
Stanford:	The judges sit not here to make disputations, but to declare the law, which hath been sufficiently done, if you would consider it.
Hare:	You have heard reason and the law, if you will conceive it.
Throckmorton:	Oh merciful God, oh eternal Father, which seest all things, what manner of proceedings are these? To what purpose serveth the statute of repeal the last parliament, where I heard some of you here present, and divers other of the queen's learned counsel, grievously inveigh against the cruel and bloody laws of king Henry the eighth, and against some laws made in my late sovereign lord and master's time, king Edward the sixth. Some termed them "Draco's laws,"[62] which were written in blood. Some said they were more intolerable than any laws that

---

[62] Draco's laws: Draco, archon of Athens in 621 B.C., author of a a severe code of laws; hence "draconian law."

Dionysius[63] or any other tyrant made. In conclusion, as many men, so many bitter terms and names those laws had. And, moreover, the preface of the same statute doth recite that, for words only, many great personages and others of good behaviour have been most cruelly cast away by these former sanguinolent thirsty laws, with many other suggestions for the repeal of the same. And now let us put on indifferent eyes, and thoroughly consider with ourselves, as you the judges handle the constructions of the statute of Edward the third, with your equity and extensions, whether we be not in much worse case now than we were when those cruel laws yoked us. These laws, albeit they were grievous and captious, yet they had the very property of a law after Saint Paul's description.[64] For those laws did admonish us, and discover our sins plainly unto us, and when a man is warned, he is half armed. These laws, as they be handled, be very baits to catch us, and only prepared for the same, and no laws. For at the first sight they ascertain us we be delivered from our old bondage, and by the late repeal the last parliament we live in more security. But when it pleaseth the higher powers to call any man's life and sayings in question, then there be constructions, interpretations, and extensions reserved to the justices and the judges' equity, [so] that the party tryable, as I am now, shall find himself in much worse case than before, when those cruel laws stood in force. Thus our amendment is from God's blessing into the warm sun. But I require you, honest men which are to try my life, consider these

---

[63] Dionysius: Dionysius I or II, tyrants of Syracuse from 405 to 339 B.C.

[64] Saint Paul's description: in Romans 7:7: "I had not known sin, but by the law." Throckmorton is calmly misapplying Pauline doctrine here. Paul's purpose was to solve the dilemma caused by the dictum that the old Law was abrogated by the Gospel, and to maintain respect for Jewish law in the Christian community. Thus he argued that law supplies the conscience, which can otherwise only vaguely apprehend the nature of sin, with formal definitions of the forbidden.

opinions of my life. Judges be rather agreeable to the time than to the truth; for their judgements be repugnant to their own principle, repugnant to their godly and best learned predecessors' opinions, repugnant, I say, to the proviso in the statute of repeal made in the last parliament.

Attorney: Master Throckmorton, quiet your self, and it shall be the better for you.

Throckmorton: Master Attorney, I am not so unquiet as you be, and yet our cases are not alike. But because I am so tedious to you, and have long troubled this presence, it may please my lord Chief Justice to repeat the evidence wherewith I am charged, and my answers to all the objections, if there be no other matter to lay against me.

Then the Chief Justice remembered particularly all the depositions and evidences given against the prisoner, and either for want of good memory, or good will, the prisoner's answers were in part not recited; whereupon the prisoner craved indifferency, and did help the judge's old memory with his own recital.

Sendall: My masters of the jury, you have to enquire whether Sir Nicholas Throckmorton, knight, here prisoner at the bar, be guilty of these treasons, or any of them, whereof he hath been indicted and this day arraigned, yea or no. And if you find him guilty, you shall inquire what lands, tenements, goods, and chattels he had at the day of his treasons committed, or at any time since; and whether he fled for the treasons or no, if you find him not guilty.

Throckmorton: Have you said what is to be said?

Sendall: Yea, for this time.

Throckmorton: Then, I pray you, give me leave to speak a few words to the jury. The weight and gravity of my cause hath greatly occasioned me to trouble you here long, and therefore I mind not to entertain you here long with any prolix oration. You perceive, notwithstanding, this day great contention betwixt the judges and the queen's learned counsel on the one party, and me the poor and woeful prisoner on the other party. The trial of our whole controversy, the trial of my innocency, the trial of my life, lands and goods, and the destruction of my posterity for ever, doth rest in your good judgements. And albeit many this day have greatly inveighed against me, the final determination thereof is transferred only to you. How grievous and horrible the shedding of innocents' blood is in the sight of almighty God, I trust you do remember. Therefore take heed (I say) for Christ's sake, do not defile your consciences with such heinous and notable crimes. They be grievously and terribly punished, as in this world and vale of misery upon the children's children to the third and fourth generation, and in the world to come with everlasting fire and damnation. Lift up your minds to God, and care not too much for the world, look not back to the fleshpots of Egypt, which will allure you from heavenly respects to worldly security, and can thereof neither make you any surety. Believe, I pray you, the queen and her magistrates be more delighted with favorable equity than with rash cruelty. And in that you be all citizens, I will take my leave of you with St. Paul's farewell to the Ephesians.[65] Citizens also you be, whom he took to record that he was pure from shedding any blood, a special token and doctrine left for your instruction, that every of you may wash his hands of innocents' blood shed, when you shall take your leave of this wretched world. The Holy Ghost be amongst you.

---

[65] Paul's farewell to the Ephesians: Ephesians 6:10–20. These unspoken verses were a famous admonition to the Christian community to maintain solidarity: "For we wrestle not against flesh and blood, but against principalities, against powers, against the rulers of the darkness of this world, against spiritual wickedness in high places."

Sendall:	Come hither, Sergeant, take the jury with you, and suffer no man to come at them, but to be ordered as the law appointeth, until they be agreed upon their verdict.
Throckmorton:	It may please you, my lords and masters which be commissioners, to give order that no person have access or conference with the jury, neither that any of the queen's learned counsel be suffered to repair to them, or to talk with any of them, until they present themselves here in open court, to publish their verdict.

Upon the prisoner's suit on this behalf, the Bench gave order that two sergeants were sworn to suffer no man to repair to the jury, until they were agreed according unto order. Whereupon then the prisoner was by commandment of the Bench withdrawn from the bar, and the court adjourned until three of the clock at afternoon, at which hour the commissioners returned to the Guildhall, and there did tarry until the jury were agreed upon the verdict. And about five of the clock, their agreement being advertised to the commissioners, the said prisoner Sir Nicholas Throckmorton was again brought to the bar, where also the jury did repair; and being demanded whether they were agreed upon their verdict, answered universally with one voice, "Yea." Then it was asked who should speak for them. They answered, "Whetston, the foreman."

Sendall:	Nicholas Throckmorton, knight, hold up thy hand.

Then the prisoner did so upon the summons.

Sendall:	You that be of the jury, look upon the prisoner.

The jury did as they were enjoined.

Sendall:	How say you, is Master Throckmorton, knight, there prisoner at the bar, guilty of the treasons whereof he hath been indicted and arraigned in manner and form, yea or no?
Whetston:	No.
Sendall:	How say you, did he fly upon them?

Whetston:	No, we find no such thing.
Throckmorton:	I had forgotten to answer that question before, but you have found according to truth; and for the better warranty of your doings, understand that I came to London, and so to the queen's counsel unbrought, when I understood that they demanded for me; and yet I was almost an hundred miles hence, where if I had not presumed upon my truth, I could have withdrawn myself from catching.
Bromley:	How say you the rest of you, is Whetston's verdict all your verdicts.
Jury:	*The whole inquest answered Yea.*
Bromley:	Remember yourselves better. Have you considered substantially the whole evidence in sort as it was declared and recited. The matter doth touch the queen's highness, and yourselves also. Take good heed what you do.
Whetston:	My lord, we have thoroughly considered the evidence laid against the prisoner, and his answers to all these matters, and accordingly we have found him not guilty, agreeable to all our consciences.
Bromley:	If you have done well, it is the better for you.
Throckmorton:	It is better to be tried, than to live suspected. Blessed be the Lord God of Israel, for he hath visited and redeemed his people, and hath raised up a mighty salvation for us in the house of his servant David.[66] And it may please you, my lord Chief Justice, forsomuch as I have been indicted and arraigned of sundry treasons, and have according to the law put my trial to God and my country, that is to say, to these honest men which have found me not guilty, I humbly beseech you give me such

---

[66] Here Throckmorton audaciously cites Luke 1:68–9, Zachariah's prophecy of the birth of John the Baptist.

benefit, acquittal and judgement as the law in this case doth appoint.

When the prisoner had said these words the commissioners consulted together.

Throckmorton: May it please you, my lord Chief Justice, to pronounce sentence for my discharge?

Bromley: Whereas you do ask the benefit that the law in such case doth appoint, I will give it you; to wit, that where you have been indicted of sundry high treasons, and have been here this day before the queen's commissioners and justices arraigned of the said treasons, whereunto you have pleaded "Not Guilty," and have for trial therein put yourself on God and your country, and they have found you not guilty, the court doth award that you be clearly discharged, paying your fees. Notwithstanding, Master Lieutenant, take him with you again, for there are other matters to charge him withall.

Throckmorton: It may please you, my lords and masters of the queen's highness' Privy Council, to be on my behalf humble suitors to her majesty, that like as the law this day (God be praised) hath purged me of the treasons wherewith I was most dangerously charged; so it might please her excellent majesty to purge me in her private judgement, and both forgive and forget my over rash boldness, that I used in talk of her highness's marriage with the prince of Spain, matters too far above my capacity, and I very unable to consider the gravity thereof, a matter impertinent for me a private person to talk of, which did appertain to her highness's Privy Council to have in deliberation. And if it shall please her highness of her bountiful liberality to remit my former oversights, I shall think myself happy for the trial of the danger that I have this day escaped, and may thereby admonish me to eschew things above my reach, and also to instruct me to deal with matters agreeable to my vocation. And God save the queen's majesty, and grant the same long to reign over us. And the same Lord be praised for you, the magistrates, before whom I have had my trial this day indifferently by the law, and you have proceeded with me accordingly; and the grace of God be amongst you now and ever.

There was no answer made by any of the Bench to the prisoner's suit, but the attorney did speak these words:

Attorney: And it please you, my lords, forsomuch as it seemeth that these men of the jury, which have strangely acquitted the prisoner of his treasons whereof he was indicted, will forthwith depart the court, I pray you for the queen, that they, and every of them, may be bound in a recognisance of five hundred pounds apiece, to answer to such matters as they shall be charged with in the queen's behalf, whensoever they shall be charged or called.

Whetston: I pray you, my lords, be good to us, and let us not be molested for discharging our consciences truly. We be poor merchantmen and have great charge upon our hands, and our livings do depend upon our travels; therefore it may please you to appoint us a certain day for our appearance, for perhaps some of us may be in foreign parts about our business.

Appendix A

The Legend of Sir Nicholas Throckmorton

First published under this title by Francis Peck in 1736, the poem was re-edited by J.G. Nichols in 1874, who preferred to call it "The Ghost of Sir Nicholas Throckmorton." Since the author describes how this ghost brings him a warning from beyond the grave, "sith I thy Uncle am," Peck arbitrarily identified him as Sir Thomas Throckmorton, son of Robert. Nichols briefly considered the claims of Job, son of Clement, but then decided, equally arbitrarily, in favor of John, son of Anthony. The choice is not meaningless, since Thomas was a staunch Catholic, and John had no obvious experiences that would fit him for the part. By far the most likely candidate is Job Throckmorton, an ardent Protestant, who became in 1586 an outspoken member of parliament for Warwick. Throckmorton delivered three inflammatory speeches in the Commons, and then had to flee London to escape imprisonment in the Tower, going into hiding in his sister's house at Hillingdom, near Uxbridge. Deprived of a parliamentary forum, he began publishing the notorious Marprelate pamphlets, several of which had a legal focus and a particular interest in the English statutes. The uncle arrives "young hare-brain'd heads to guide," and the notorious Job would be a good candidate for such cautions. If this were so, 1587 would be a plausible *terminus a quo* for the writing of the poem. Even though he was over forty at the time of his disgrace and flight, in the letter of apology that he wrote to Burghley on April 3, 1587, Job refers to his behavior as "rashness" and suggests that it was the privilege of free speech allowed in the Commons that was "apt enough to bring a young head into a distemperature."[1] In addition, Job's letter to Burghley admits that he "had read indeed long ago, but..never felt it by experience till now: That th'indignation of the Prince was death"; and the poem speaks of

---

[1] See Leland H. Carlson, *Martin Marprelate, Gentleman: Master Job Throkmorton laid open in his colors* (San Marino, 1981), 103–08, 193–96, 342.

how the Throckmorton brothers had striven to please Henry VIII, "Whose wrath is worse than death, by man's account," (Stanza 35).

Only a few of the 229 stanzas are reprinted here, chosen for their relevance to the trial and the significance it apparently held for this late sixteenth-century reader, the author of the *Legend*. Particularly noteworthy is his insistence (echoing Bradford's) that the reader consult the trial transcript in the "Chronicle," which in 1587 had just been republished (as also, coincidentally, had *The Mirror for Magistrates*).

Stanza 2:

[I] heard him say, "Who know not, warning need;
Young years are prone in slippery ways to slide.
Attend my words, and let them stand in stead
Of beaten path young hare-brained heads to guide.
Thou hopest by hap some favour for to find;
But all in vain, thou sail'st against the wind."

Stanza 6:

Aghast I stared; my hair did stand upright,
For all the space he held me by the arm.
The sentence hard, but stranger seemed the sight,
Till by the words I knew he meant no harm.
"Abandon dread," quoth he, "for good I came,
Assure thyself, sith I thy uncle am."

Stanza 8:

"The monster kept in labyrinth slew all
Save only him who had the clue of thread.
Thou canst not pass one year without a fall,
Unless thou tak'st that counsel which I bid.
A warning may show thee to set thy feet
That in the end thou need'st not them to fleet.[2]

Stanza 112: (upon Edward VI's death)

"And though I liked not the religion
Which all her life Queene Mary had professed.
Yet in my mind that wicked motion
Right heirs to displace I did detest.
Causeless to proffer any injury
I meant it not, but sought for remedy.

---

[2] To fleet: to fly or run away.

Stanza 113:

"Wherefore from four of us the news was sent,
How that her brother he was dead and gone.
In post her goldsmith then from London went,
By whom the message was dispatched anon.
She asked [him] if we knew it certainly,
Who said, "Sir Nicholas knew it verily.""

Stanza 114:

"The author bred the errand's great mistrust.
She feared a train to lead her to a trap.
She said, if Robert had been there, she durst
Have gaged her life, and hazarded the hap.
Her letter made, she knew not what to do.
She sent them out, but not subscribed thereto.[3]

Stanza 115:

"When first the Queen was crowned I lived well;
But Spaniards came, and Wyatt quickly rose;
Who only meant outlandish force to quell.
To him adherent men did me suppose.
When he had played his woeful tragedy,
Then next ensued my bitter comedy.[4]

Stanza 122:

"Because the Chronicle doth show at large
My accusation and acquittal both,
I mean thereby to ease me of that charge,
Lest that my being tedious thou dost loathe.
Yet read it, when thou hast convenient leisure.
Perhaps my passed pain shall bring thee pleasure.

Stanza 123:

"There shalt thou view a precedent most rife,
How I, arraigned of treason, was set free
By jurors' verdict, not to lose my life.
The only *a per se*[5] of my degree;

---

[3] Not subscribed thereto: without her signature.

[4] Compare Throckmorton's own use of dramatic terminology. It is worth noting that the *Legend* regards the trial as comedic.

[5] *A per se*: the first, best or unique person or thing.

I mean, that was but of Gentility,
Yet few have scaped of Nobility.

Stanza 124:

The plunge once past, then was I back again
To Tower led; where I remained a year,
And heard that me once more they would arraign.
Which sure, I thought, would touch me very near.
But since that passed[6] laws of equity,
Amongst the rest I went at liberty.

Stanza 129:

"For lo! the man who lent me law of late[7]
To save my life and put himself in danger,
Did then advancement get to mend his state,
And next did seek appease the Prince's anger,
Whose heavy wrath, he knew, was bent on me;
But yet at length from that he set me free.

Stanza 130:

"In time himself shall stand as much in need
To have some help, and then shall wish for me.
But sure his case I rue. My heart doth bleed
To think of that which thou thyself shall see,
How he by wrongful means, for doing right,
Shall justice have, devoid of mercy quite.

---

[6] Passed: exceeded what the law allowed; i.e. the principle of double jeopardy.

[7] The *Legend* is our only source for this important detail, implying that someone smuggled lawbooks into the Tower to assist Sir Nicholas in his defence. Since this man appears, by the poem's structure, to be also the brother who interceded for Sir Nicholas during his precautionary self-exile in France, the most reasonable candidate is not the eldest brother Robert, but rather the seventh son John, who was trained as a lawyer at the Middle Temple. After having reluctantly drawn up the proclamation which named Lady Jane Grey the heir after Burghley declined to do so, he quickly made his peace with Mary, and was appointed Master of Requests. The *Legend*'s account of how Nicholas's benefactor later suffered his own legal calamity ("which thou thyself shall see") seems to have no bearing on Robert, but John, who became Justice of Chester, in 1580 was removed from his post for partiality towards his kin, fined heavily in Star Chamber, and imprisoned in the Fleet, where he may have died.

Stanza 131:

"Yet then, for my avail, (who hid my face
From Prince's sight) my brother did not let
To sue, till she received me to her grace,
And said all former faults she did forget,
And eke forgive; so I returned again.
I mercy craved; I mercy did obtain.

Stanza 132:

"I thus acknowledge that beyond my reach
I intermeddled with the Prince's state..
My betters did I go about to teach.
To Spaniards I did bear a mortal hate.
My mind was bent to let their coming in.
I tell a troth; dissembling is a sin.

Stanza 180:

"Hereafter, one of mine shall hope his harm,
And speak too soon the thing his heart would wish.
But wit too dearly bought his tongue shall charm,
Whose fault shall oft be layed in his dish;
And he shall know that cold and malice take
More suddenly than any they forsake.

Stanza 228:

"Wherefore, sith burned child may well his friend
Beware, lest he be scorched in flaming fire,
I wish thou shouldst thine errors late amend,
And from those dangerous thoughts thyself retire.
Diogenes lived safely in his cell,
And thou, in Littleton,[8] mayst safely dwell."

---

[8] Littleton: Peck assumed this to be a place-name. Alternatively it could simply mean "in the common law," for which Littleton's *Tenures* commonly stood.

Appendix B

Tudor documents relating to Throckmorton's trial

I. John Bradford, *Remarks on a memorable trial*, from Emmanuel College Library, Cambridge, Ms. 2.2.15, no. 98; first reprinted in *The Writings of John Bradford ... Martyr, 1555*, ed. Aubrey Townsend, 2 vols.,(Cambridge: Cambridge University Press, 1848), 1:405–07.

These remarks, which appear to be intended as a preface to a published edition of the trial, imply that it had *not* been published by the spring of 1555, when Bradford was in prison in London awaiting execution for heresy, but suggest that it may very well have been published later in that year, after his burning on June 30. In the *Remarks*, Bradford explains that he has been "lent" a manuscript copy of the "book," and has evidently written his preface to the Throckmorton trial in the manuscript itself. When he was first imprisoned in the Tower, in February 1554, he shared a room with Cranmer, Latimer and Ridley, since the prison was overcrowded owing to Wyatt's rebellion. The interest of his *Remarks* resides in Bradford's concern to extend the trial's readership, beyond the radical Protestant community of which he was a member to the entire educated class, "the nobility and gentlemen of England." His repeated injunction, "Read this book," and his analysis of Throckmorton's own education in scripture and "the statutes, laws, and chronicles," closely matches the educational agenda of Holinshed's *Chronicles* as I understand it.

1555. This Preface was made in *anno Domini* 1555.

To the reader John Bradford wisheth grace, mercy, peace, and increase of all godly knowledge and life.

    After this book came to my hands, as I was in prison for the testimony of the Lord, I could not but read the same to see how the Lord assisted his servant that put his trust in him: which thing I thank God I did so see, that I could not but think myself bound to help what I could by my testimony, to allure all others by this book thereunto. And therefore I, being a poor man of vile state and condition concerning this world, and of learning unmeet of place in any book for my name, have presumed by a godly presumption, tending to do good to all men and hurt to no man, to write thus much in behalf of this book, that it is worthy to be had in print, and diligently read of all men, but especially of the nobility and gentlemen of England: whose houses and names could not but continue, if that yet now they would begin to take this gentleman a sampler to ensue, and a pattern to press after. For here thou, good reader, shalt perceive a gentleman in deed, and not in name only: his trust was in the Lord, and not in man, and therefore he was not confounded: he honoured God, and therefore God hath honoured him accordingly. His study was in God's word, and therefore found he comfort: by it he found more wisdom and had more knowledge than all his enemies, which were not few nor foolish to the judgement of the world. They came to him as Goliah the mighty giant, harnessed and armed cap-a-pie: he came as a little David with his sling, and had the victory. In this weak man thou mayest see God's power, presence, wisdom, and goodness, to occasion thee to put thy trust in the Lord, and to hang altogether upon him, who in the evil day will deliver them that fear him. What wisdom, what grace, what audacity, did God give to him in his need! What could all the learned lawyers, which better might be termed lewd losels[9] of the realm, do against him? What could all the power of the queen's highness prevail? Such a thing it is to trust in the Lord, to fear him, and to be a godly student of his word, as doubtless it appeareth this good man was. Who would not serve such a God, as can in despite of all his enemies triumph over them by his simple servant?

Read the book, and thou shalt see what knowledge this gentleman had in the statutes, laws, and chronicles of the realm, to teach the nobility and gentlemen, which are and would be magistrates and rulers of the realm, to spend more time to attain wisdom and knowledge to execute their offices than they now do. Read this book, and thou shalt see what false packing there is against the simple and plain truth. Read this book, and thou shalt see how unrighteousness sitteth in place of justice. Read this book, and thou shalt see how truth is defaced, and falsehood maintained. Read this book, and thou shalt see how perilous a thing it is to testify the truth.

---

[9] "Losels," worthless persons, lost to humanity.

The good men empanelled of the quest shall tell the same. A greater honour never came to the city of London than by those twelve men. What said I, to the city of London? Nay, to the whole realm of England: for, alas! if they had not more conscience and truth than king, queen, lords, counsellors, judges, sergeants, attornies, solicitors, lawyers, &c., England had been guilty of innocent blood; as alas, alas! it is to be feared too much thereof crieth for vengeance. Lord, spare us, and have mercy upon us.

But what reward had this good jury? Well, I pass over that: a papistical reward. What is that? Forsooth, such as Julianus Apostata[10] gave to the faithful Christians.

God our Father look better on this gear in his good time, which in respect of his enemies is at hand; "for they have scattered abroad his law." O that amongst us, who pretend to be God's friends, were true repentance! Then might we say: "*Tempus est ut miserearis, Domine*: It is time, O Lord, to show mercy upon us."[11] God do so for his holy name's sake! Amen.

Thus much I was so bold to scribble in this book, being lent unto me, because I would occasion some men of authority and learning to commend it, as it is most worthy.

E carcere,
JOHN BRADFORD.

II. Rose (Hickman) Throckmorton's autobiography; British Library Additional Ms. 43827A, fols. 1–18v. Two other manuscript copies exist, Add. Ms. 43827B, and Add. Ms. 45027. It has been reprinted several times, most recently by Maria Dowling and Joy Shakespeare as "Religion and Politics in mid Tudor England through the eyes of an English Protestant Woman: the Recollections of Rose Hickman," in *Bulletin of the Institute of Historical Research*, 55 (1982), 94–102.

Only two sections of the autobiography relate to the Throckmorton trial; the opening paragraph, where Rose describes an act of courage in defence of Protestantism performed by her father, William Locke, which was recorded in Holinshed's *Chronicles*, a record which she takes as a model for her own; and the paragraph in which she describes the interaction between her own family and the Throckmorton jurors, as well as providing us with their later history. The interest of this

---

[10] Flavius Claudius Julianus (called the "Apostate") was Roman Emperor 361–3; he was distinguished for his persecution of Christians.

[11] Psalm 119, 126.

document resides in its witness to the solidarity between the London merchants who had converted to Protestantism, the role of mercantile wealth in mitigating the effects of religious persecution, and the suggestion that those in high places had interceded for the jurors, to transfer them from the Fleet to more commodious quarters in the Treasurer's house. Possibly the "great means" used was the influence of the Treasurer himself.

Certain old stories recorded by an aged gentlewoman a time before her death, to be perused by her children and posterity. Written by her with her hand in the 85th year of age, and about the year our lord 1610.

Of my father. In Holinshed's chronicle I find this story. In the 25th year of King Henry the 8, being the year of our Lord 1534, at the suit of the Lady Katherine, dowager, a curse was sent from the pope which cursed both the king and the realm. This curse was set up in the town of Dunkirk in Flanders; for the bringer thereof durst no nearer approach; where it was taken down by William Locke of London, mercer. Now I his daughter, Rose Throckmorton, widow, late wife of Simon Throckmorton, esquire, and first the wife of Anthony Hickman, a merchant of London, reading this of my father, have thought good to leave to my children this addition to it. ...

When Queen Mary came to the crown the idolatrous Mass was set up with public profession of popery throughout this realm, and cruel persecution of those good Christians that in a good conscience refused to yield themselves to that idolatry. At which time we did receive into our house in the city of London divers godly and well disposed Christians that were desirous to shelter themselves from the cruel persecution of those times. And we and they did table together in a chamber, keeping the doors close for fear of the promoters, as we read in the gospel the disciples of Christ did for fear of the Jews.[12] And thus we kept our house in London in the beginning of Queen Mary's days. But then there came forth a very strict proclamation, enjoining all to come to church and receive the sacrament after the popish fashion; after which proclamation we durst no longer keep our house, but my husband [Anthony Hickman] used means to convey away the preachers and other good Christians (that were in our house) beyond sea, giving them money to supply their wants. ...

Then my good husband was accused to the high commissioners for the conveying away and relieving those good Christians, whom the

---

[12] John 20:19.

high commissioners called the queen's enemies, and for not conform-
ing himself to popery, according to the queen's injunctions, and for the
same my husband and my brother (who was also accused with him)
were committed to close prison in the Fleet. And during the time of
their imprisonment they could not be suffered to have any private
conference together, neither could any other be suffered to have
conference with either of them. But they were kept in several rooms in
the prison, and were often severally examined, and when either of them
was examined the commissioners would endeavour to make him believe
that the other had confessed as much as they would have drawn from
him, and thereupon they would advise him to confess as his brother
had done before him. But nevertheless there was not much gotten forth
of their own confession by that means, although indeed there was a
collection of 40 marks a week duly collected and exhibited by my
husband and brother with some other well disposed merchants to the
relief of the distressed ministry, about which my husband and brother
were sore charged in their examinations. And at the same time there
was also in the Fleet the jury that acquitted Sir Nicholas Throckmorton
upon his arraignment of high treason, who because they chose rather
to discharge their consciences by finding him not guilty, than to please
the commissioners and judges that sat upon his trial by finding him
guilty contrary to their consciences were committed to the Fleet, but so
as they had the liberty of the prison. And these jurymen, being all
merchants of London, had compassion upon the distress of my husband
and brother; for these jurymen having the liberty that was wanting to
my husband and brother in the prison, would come under the chamber
window where my brother was, and under the chamber window where
my husband was, and talk aloud to one another, to the end that my
husband and brother might hear them, what they heard touching any
of the matters for which my husband and brother were questioned, and
so by that means gave them light of many things before their examinations.

Afterwards by great means that was made for them they were
removed from the Fleet to the house of the Marquess of Winchester
who was then Lord Treasurer,[13] but were also there kept in several
rooms as close prisoners, not being suffered to come together but by
stealth, when the marquess was at dinner or gone abroad. Then they
procured to themselves liberty to come together by giving gratuities to
the gentlemen that attended about the house. And whilst they were thus
detained prisoners, there came to the court the lord of Barrow in the

---

[13] Sir William Paulet, Lord St. John.

Low Countries,[14] who became a great suitor for their enlargements, in regard of the want that his country had of their trading and merchandise. And partly by his means, and partly by the Lord Treasurer's favour (which we purchased with chests of sugar and pieces of velvet to the value of £200 or thereabouts) they were (after long imprisonment) set at liberty.

III. Sir Thomas Smith, *The Commonwealth of England and Manner of Government Thereof compiled by the honorable Sir Thomas Smith ... one of the principal secretaries unto two most worthy Princes, King Edward and Queen Elizabeth.* (London: John Windet, 1589).

This important work of constitutional and legal description was written ca. 1565, but not published until 1583, six years after Smith's death. It has a complicated history of reprinting and revision during Elizabeth's reign, as also of overlap with the second edition of Holinshed's *Chronicles* (1587). Only those passages are here cited which explain Tudor court procedure, including an obvious reference to the fate of the Throckmorton jury.

Book 2, Chapter 10: Of Pleas or Actions:
Pleas or Actions criminal be in English called pleas of the crown, which be all those which tend to take away a man's life or any member of him, for his evil deserving against the prince and commonwealth.

And this name is given not without a cause. For taking this for a principle, that the life and member of an Englishmen is in the power only of the prince and his laws, when any of his subjects is spoiled either of life or member, the prince is endamaged thereby, and hath good cause to ask account how his subjects should come to that mischief. And again, for so much as the prince who governeth the sceptre, and holdeth the crown of England, hath this in his care and charge, to see the realm well governed, the life, members and possessions of his subjects kept in peace and assurance: he that by violence shall attempt to break that peace and assurance hath forfeited against the sceptre and crown of England; and therefore not without a cause in all inquisitions and indictments, if any be found by the 12 men to have offended in that behalf, straight the prince is said to be party, and he that shall speak for the prisoner is rebuked, as speaking against the prince. Nevertheless it is never defended, but the prisoner and party

---

[14] Jean de Glymes, marquis de Berghes and lord of Bergen-op-Zoom, who was in London in March 1554.

defendant in any cause may allege for himself all the reasons, means and defences that he can, and shall be peaceably heard and quietly. But in those pleas or pursuits of the crown, procurer or advocate he gets none, which in civil and pecuniary matters ... is never denied.

Chapter 17: Of the 12 Men:
... The sheriff always warneth 24 to appear, lest peradventure any might be sick or have a just cause of absence ... 12 they must be at the least to make an inquest or as some call it a quest. ... Either party when they be come taketh their challenges against so many of them as they will, which be that he may not spend so much land a year, he is allied, feed or servant to his adverse party, he is his enemy, &c. ... When the quest is full, they be sworn to declare the truth of that issue, according to the evidence and their conscience. Then the sergeants of either side[15] declare the issue, and each for his client sayeth as much as he can. Evidences of writings be showed, witnesses be sworn and heard before them, not after the fashion of the civil law but openly, that not only the twelve, but the judges, the parties and as many as be present may hear what each witness doth say. ... When it is thought that it is enough pleaded before them, and the witnesses have said what they can, one of the judges with a brief and pithy recapitulation reciteth to the twelve in sum the arguments ..., that which the witnesses have declared, and the chief points of the evidence showed in writing, and once again putteth them in mind of the issue, ... and biddeth them go together. Then there is a bailiff charged with them to keep them in a chamber not far off, without bread, drink, light or fire until they be agreed, that is, till they all agree upon one verdict concerning the same issue and upon one among them who shall speak for them all when they be agreed; for it goeth not by the most part, but each man must agree. They return and in so few words as may be they give their determination: few I call six or seven, or eight words at the most (for commonly the issue is brought so narrow, that such number of words may be enough to affirm or to deny it) which done they are dismissed to go whither they will. The party with whom they have given their sentence giveth the inquest their dinner that day most commonly, and this is all that they have for their labor, notwithstanding that they come some 20, some 30 or 40 miles or more to the place where they give their verdict. All the rest is of their own charge.

---

[15] This is a description of procedure in civil actions, but except for the reference to "adverse parties" it applies to criminal actions also.

Chapter 25: Of … the definitive proceedings in causes criminal:
… There the clerk speaketh first to one of the prisoners: A.B. come to
the bar, hold up thy hand. The clerk goeth on: A.B. thou by the name
of A.B. of such a town, in such a county, are indicted, that. … What
sayest thou to it, art thou guilty or not guilty? If he will not answer, or
not answer directly, guilty or not guilty, after he hath been once or twice
so interrogated, he is judged mute, that is, dumb by contumacy,[16] and
his condemnation is to be pressed to death, which is one of the cruellest
deaths that may be. He is laid upon a table, and another laid upon him,
and so much weight of stones or lead laid upon that table, while as his
body be crushed, and his life by that violence taken from him. This
death some strong and stouthearted man doth choose, for, being not
condemned of felony, his blood is not corrupted, his lands nor goods
confiscate to the Prince, which in all cases of felony are commonly lost
from him and his heirs, if he be forejudged, that is, condemned for a
felon by the law. If he confess the indictment to be true, then when he
is arraigned no twelve men goeth upon him. There resteth but the
judge's sentence of the pain of death.

If he plead Not Guilty, as commonly all thieves, robbers and mur-
derers do, though they have confessed the fact before the justice of the
peace that examined them, though they be taken with the manner,
which in Latin they call *in flagranti crimine*, howsoever it be, if he
plead there Not Guilty, the clerk asketh him how he will be tried, and
telleth him he must say, "By God and the Country," for these be the
words formal of his trial after indictment, and where the Prince is party.
If the prisoner do say so, "I will be tried by God and the Country," then
the clerk replieth: "… Lo, these honest men that be come here, be in
the place and stead of the Country: and if thou hast any thing to say to
[i.e. against] any of them, look upon them well and now speak, for thou
standest upon thy life and death. Then calleth he in the first juror: B.C.
come to the book, and so giveth him an oath to go uprightly between
the Prince and the prisoner, &c. If the prisoner objecteth nothing
against him, he calleth another, and so another, till there be 12 or above:
and for the most part the prisoner can say nothing against them, for
they are chosen but for that day, and are unknown to him, nor they
know not him, nor they know not him, as I said being substantial
yeomen that dwell about the place … or near where the felony is
supposed to be committed, men acquainted with daily labour and
travail, and not with such idle persons as be ready to do such mischiefs.

---

[16] By contumacy: out of stubbornness.

... At their departing, they have in writing nothing given them but the indictment, the clerk repeating to them the effect of it, and showing more that if they find him guilty, they shall inquire what goods, lands and tenements the said person had at the time of the felony committed; ... If they find him not guilty, they shall inquire whether he fled for the felony or no.

... By that time that the inquests for the prisoners be dispatched, it is commonly dinner time, the judges and justices go to dinner, and after dinner return to the same place. ... The inquests have no sooner agreed upon their charge one way or other, but they tell the bailiff and pray to be heard, and considering that they be themselves all this while as prisoners as I said before, it is no marvel though they make expedition.

Book 3, Chapter 1: Of that which in other countries is called appellation, or provocation, to amend the judgement or sentence definitive, which is thought unjustly given in causes criminal.

... if having pregnant evidence nevertheless the twelve do acquit the malefactor, which they will do sometimes, and especially if they perceive either one of the justices, or of the judges, or some other man to pursue too much and too maliciously the death of the prisoner, or do suspect some subornation of the witness or of them which do give evidence; and sometime if they perceive the judge would have the prisoner escape, and in repeating the evidence do give them thereof some watchword. But if they do (as I have said) pronounce Not Guilty upon the prisoner against whom manifest witness is brought in, the prisoner escapeth; but the twelve not only be rebuked by the judges, but also threatened of punishment, and many times commanded to appear in the Star Chamber, or before the Privy Council, for the matter. But this threatening chanceth oftener than the execution thereof, and the twelve answer with most gentle words, they did according to their consciences, and pray the judges to be good unto them, they did as they thought right, and as they accorded all, and so it passeth away for the most part. Yet I have seen in my time (but not in the reign of the Queen now) that an inquest, for pronouncing one Not Guilty of treason contrary to such evidence as was brought in, were not only imprisoned for a space, but a huge fine set upon their heads, which they were fain to pay. ... But those doings were even then of very many accounted very violent, tyrannical, and contrary to the liberty and custom of the realm of England. Wherefore it commeth very seldom in use, yet so much at a time the inquest may be corrupted, that the Prince may have cause with justice to punish them; for they are men, and subject to corruption and partiality, as others be.

Textual Note

The *Trial of Sir Nicholas Throckmorton* is edited from Raphael Holinshed, *The Chronicles of England, Scotland, and Ireland* (London, 1587), a revision and expansion of the first edition of 1577. An unannotated and occasionally inaccurate text is also available in *Holinshed's Chronicles of England, Scotland and Ireland*, ed. Henry Ellis, 6 vols. (London: J. Johnson et al., 1807–8; repr. with an introduction by Vernon Snow, New York: AMS Press, 1965), 4:31–64. Unlike many sections of Mary Tudor's reign, the account of the trial was not altered or supplemented in the 1587 version (with the exception of one marginal comment). It was possibly based on a pamphlet published surreptitiously shortly after the trial, which has now disappeared, but whose typographical features were reproduced in the *Chronicles*.

The *Trial* apparently circulated in manuscript also. Surviving copies are:

1. British Library. Stowe Ms. 280, fol. 75 ff.

2. Bodleian Library, Oxford. Ms. Rawlinson C. 408.

3. "A Quarto Vol. The Order of the arraignment of Sir Nicholas Throgmorton" listed by the Historical Manuscripts Commission as at Helmingham Hall, Suffolk, the property of Baron Tollemache, has now disappeared into other private hands.

Select Bibliography

Allen, Cardinal William. *A brief historie of the glorious martyrdom of xii reverend priests*, ed. J.H. Pollen. London: Burns & Oates, 1908.

Bellamy, John. *The Law of Treason in the later Middle Ages*. Cambridge: Cambridge University Press, 1970.

———, *The Tudor Law of Treason*. London: Routledge and Kegan Paul, 1989.

Beer, Barrell L. *Northumberland: the Political Career of John Dudley, Earl of Warwick and Duke of Northumberland*. Kent, Ohio: Kent State University Press, 1973.

Bowler, Gerry, "Marian Protestants and the Idea of Violent Resistance to Tyranny," in *Protestantism and the National Church in Sixteenth Century England*, ed. Peter Lake and Maria Dowling. New York: Croom Helm, 1987, pp. 124–43.

Brigden, Susan. *London and the Reformation*. Oxford: Clarendon Press, 1989.

Campbell, Lily B., ed. *The Mirror for Magistrates*. Cambridge: Cambridge University Press, 1938.

Carlson, Leland H. *Martin Marprelate, Gentleman: Master Job Throkmorton laid open in his colors*. San Marino: Huntington Library, 1981.

Castanien, Anne. "Censorship and Historiography in Elizabethan England: The Expurgation of Holinshed's *Chronicles*. Unpublished Ph.D, U of California, Davis, 1970.

Collinson, Patrick. *The Birthpangs of Protestant England: Religion and Cultural Change in the Sixteenth and Seventeenth Centuries*. New York: St. Martin's Press, 1988.

Dekker, Thomas. *The Famous History of Sir Thomas Wyat*. London, 1607.

Dewar, Mary, ed. Sir Thomas Smith, *De Republica Anglorum*. Cambridge: Cambridge University Press, 1982.

Dowling, Maria and Joy Shakespeare, "Religion and Politics in mid Tudor England...the Recollections of Rose Hickman," *Bulletin of the Institute of Historical Research* 55 (1982): 94–102.

Duffy, Eamon. *The Stripping of the Altars: Traditional Religion in England 1400–1580*. New Haven: Yale University Press, 1992.

Elton, G.R. *Policy and Police: The Enforcement of the Reformation in the Age of Thomas Cromwell*. Cambridge: Cambridge University Press, 1972.

————, *The Tudor Constitution*. Cambridge: Cambridge University Press, 1960, 1982.

————, *Reform and Reformation: England, 1509–1558*. Cambridge, MA.: Harvard University Press, 1977.

Foxe, John. *The Acts and Monuments*, ed. G. Townsend, 8 vols., London: Seeley, Burnside and Seeley, 1843–9; repr. New York: AMS Press, 1965.

Gasper, Julia. *The Dragon and the Dove: The Plays of Thomas Dekker*. Oxford: Clarendon Press, 1990.

Guy, John. *Tudor England*. New York: Oxford University Press, 1988.

Haigh, Christopher. *English Reformations: Religion, Politics and Society under the Tudors*. Oxford: Oxford University Press, 1993.

Hasler, P.W., ed. *The House of Commons 1509–1558*. London: Secker & Warburg, 1982.

[Hawles, Sir John]. *Remarks upon the tryals of Edward Fitzharris, Stephen Colledge,...the Lord Russel, Collonel Sidney*. London: Jacob Tonson, 1689.

Hoak, D.E. *The King's Council in the Reign of Edward VI*. Cambridge: Cambridge University Press, 1976.

Houston, Alan Craig, *Algernon Sidney and the Republican Heritage in England and America*. Princeton: Princeton University Press, 1991.

Howell, T.B., ed. *A Complete Collection of State Trials*, 21 vols. London: R. Bagshaw, 1816.

King, John. *English Reformation Literature: The Tudor Origins of the Protestant Tradition*. Princeton: Princeton University Press, 1982.

————, *Tudor Royal Iconography: Literature and Art in an Age of Religious Crisis*. Princeton: Princeton University Press, 1989.

Kitson Clark, G. *The Critical Historian*. New York: Basic Books, 1967.

Loades, David. *Two Tudor Conspiracies*. Cambridge: Cambridge University Press, 1965.

————, *The Reign of Mary Tudor: Politics, Government, and Religion in England, 1553–1558*. London: E. Benn, 1979; repr. London: Longmans, 1991.

McMichael, Jack R. and Barbara Taft, eds. *The Writings of William Walwyn*. Athens: U of Georgia Press, 1989.

Nichols, J.G., ed. *The Chronicle of Queen Jane, and two years of Queen Mary*. London: Camden Society, 1850.

————, ed. *The Ghost of Sir Nicholas Throckmorton*. London: Roxburghe Club, 1874.

Norbrook, David, *Poetry and Politics in the English Renaissance*. London: Routledge and Kegan Paul, 1984.

Patterson, Annabel. *Reading Holinshed's Chronicles*. Chicago: Chicago University Press, 1994.

Peck, Francis. *The Legend of Sir Nicholas Throkmorton, Kt. Chief Butler of England & Chamberlain of the Exchecquer, who died of Poison, A.D. 1570, an Historical Poem: By (his Nephew) Sir Thomas Throckmorton of Littleton*; in his *New Memoirs of the life and poetical works of Mr. John Milton*. London, 1740.

Peltonen, Markku. *Classical humanism and republicanism in English political thought 1570–1640*. Cambridge: Cambridge University Press, 1995.

Rowse, A.L. *Ralegh and the Throckmortons*. London: Macmillan, 1962.

Scott, Jonathan, *Algernon Sidney and the Restoration Crisis, 1677–1683*. Cambridge: Cambridge University Press, 1991.

Sidney, Algernon, *Discourses concerning Government*, ed. Thomas Hollis, London: Andrew Millar, 1763.

Strong, Roy. *Tudor and Jacobean Portraits*. 2 vols. London, 1969.

Thorne, Samuel, ed. *Discourse upon the Exposicion & Understanding of Statutes*. San Marino: Huntington Library, 1942.

Townsend, Aubrey, ed. *The Writings of John Bradford*. Cambridge: Cambridge University Press, 1848.

Walker, Clement, ed. *The Triall of Lieut. Collonel J. Lilburne*. Southwark: H. Hills, 1649.

Wootton, David, ed. *Republicanism, Liberty, and Commercial Society, 1649–1776*. Stanford: Stanford University Press, 1994.

Index

Publications of the
Centre for Reformation and Renaissance Studies

Renaissance and Reformation Texts in Translation:
Lorenzo Valla. *The Profession of the Religious and Selections from The Falsely-Believed and Forged Donation of Constantine.* Trans. O.Z. Pugliese. 2nd ed. (1994), pp. 114

Giovanni Della Casa. *Galateo: A Renaissance Treatise on Manners.* Trans. K. Eisenbichler and K.R. Bartlett. 3rd ed. (1994), pp. 98

Bernardino Ochino. *Seven Dialogues.* Trans. R. Belladonna (1988), pp. 96

Nicholas of Cusa. *The Layman on Wisdom and The Mind.* Trans. M.L. Führer (1989), pp. 112

Andreas Karlstadt, Hieronymous Emser, Johannes Eck. *A Reformation Debate: Karlstadt, Emser, and Eck on Sacred Images.* Trans. B. Mangrum and G. Scavizzi (1998), pp. 115

Whether Secular Government Has the Right to Wield the Sword in Matters of Faith: A Controversy in Nürnberg in 1530. Trans. James M. Estes (1994), pp. 118

Jean Bodin. *On the Demon-Mania of Witches.* Abridged, trans. & ed. R.A. Scott and J.L. Pearl (1995), pp. 219

Tudor and Stuart Texts:
James I. *The True Law of Free Monarchies and Basilikon Doron.* Ed. with an intro. by D. Fischlin and M. Fortier (1996), pp. 181

The Trial of Nicholas Throckmorton. A modernized edition. Ed. with an intro. by Annabel Patterson (1998), pp. 108

Occasional Publications:
Register of Sermons Preached at Paul's Cross (1534-1642). Comp. M. MacLure. Revised by P. Pauls and J.C.Boswell (1989), pp. 151

Annotated Catalogue of Early Editions of Erasmus at the Centre for Reformation and Renaissance Studies, Toronto. Comp. J. Glomski and E. Rummel (1994), pp. 153

For additional information, contact:
CRRS Publications, Victoria University, Toronto, Ontario
M5S 1K7, CANADA
(416) 585-4484, fax (416) 585-4579,
e-mail crrs@chass.utoronto.ca